The Michigan
Estate Planning Guide
2nd Edition

D0920214

The Michigan
Estate Planning Guide
2nd Edition

The Michigan
Estate Planning Guide
2nd Edition

P. Mark Accettura, Esq.

C·O·L·L·I·N·W·O·O·D
P·R·E·S·S

The Michigan Estate Planning Guide
2nd Edition

P. Mark Accettura, Esq.

Collinwood Press
35055 W. 12 Mile Road, Suite 132
Farmington Hills, MI 48331

Cover Design and Page Layout: Deborah Rutti, Network Galleries

Cover Photo: The author (age 5), sister, Lori (age 3) and doll, "Suzie" (age unknown).

Library of Congress Catalog Number: 2002093713

Printed in the United States

International Standard Book Number: 978-0-9669278-2-5

This book is dedicated with love to my wife, Amy,
and my children: Alex, Austin, and Evan.
Many thanks to my co-workers Lynn Gross, Esq.,
Samuel Hurwitz, Esq., and Kimberly Rapp for all
of their technical help and legal insight,
and to James Knaus for his keen editing eye.

Table of Contents

Chapter 18   **109**

What income and estate tax benefits can be derived

from charitable transfers?

Chapter 19   **117**

Do I have to exhaust my assets before Medicaid

will pay my nursing home costs?

Chapter 20   **125**

My children are well-off.

Can I leave my estate to my grandchildren?

Introduction

In my twenty-plus years of practice in the estate planning area, I have learned a great deal about my craft, my clients and myself. About my clients, I have learned to listen very carefully to what they are – and what they are not – telling me. I have learned to let them tell their story. An effective estate plan requires that I understand my client's life journey, who they are, and the people who are most important to them. Important clues about their priorities, philosophies, and goals invariably emerge from our small talk.

My clients have taught me a great deal about life. After having met with more than a thousand clients, from all walks of life, I have learned that the most important things in life, in order of importance are: 1) physical and mental health; 2) a family that loves you; and 3) an upbeat positive attitude about life. I have also learned that if you compromise your health or your family to accumulate wealth, you have likely made a bad bargain. With a bit of financial planning you are not likely to be destitute in your old age, unless you lack any of the three items listed above. For these lessons I am grateful.

Few of us will leave a legacy of great wealth, authorship, or invention. Our names will never become household names to adorn buildings or stadia. Instead, we are likely to only be remembered by our closest friends, children, and grandchildren. Our estate plan is our last communication to these precious loved ones. It contains our final wishes and instructions concerning our body and possessions. We also appoint our successors to succeed us when we are no longer able – through death or disability – to manage our own affairs.

Trusts – both revocable and irrevocable – are an integral part of the modern estate plan, and are the subject of a great deal of the discussion in the Chapters that follow. Apart from avoiding probate and minimizing tax, trusts allow us to not only identify who will inherit our assets but when they will inherit them. We can essentially control from the grave to protect our surviving spouse, children, and grandchildren, as we would have done in life. We can prevent our heirs from inheriting too early, or losing their inheritance to divorce. We can encourage college attendance, and prevent handicapped children from becoming ineligible for government assistance due to their inheritance. Through trusts, we can create structures that allow our surviving spouse to manage assets after our death.

Michigan and federal law provide us with a great many tools to accomplish the estate planning results we hope to achieve. As with most things in the modern world, technical concepts and requirements abound. I have written *The Michigan Estate Planning Guide* to serve as an introduction to the concepts, terms, and tools of estate planning. I hope that it will be useful to those thinking of preparing an estate plan – as we all should – as well as to those who have already have a plan but who need to refresh their memory as to what they knew, but forgot, or perhaps what they never quite understood.

The book has been organized in a Chapter and answer format to allow you to zero in on the answer to your particular Chapter. The book can also be read like a novel – from front to back – giving the reader an overview of the entire estate planning process. I have attempted to write in clear and concise language understandable to the layperson without a legal background. Interestingly, *The Michigan Estate Planning Guide* is currently being used as a text in a number of financial planning and paralegal courses around Michigan.

Endnotes, beginning at page 131, lead professional readers, such as accountants and attorneys, to the legal authority that underpins the text. I have attempted to define terms as I go, however, you may find it useful to refer to the Glossary if a more complete definition of a term is desired.

The Chapters tend to get harder as you go. The earlier Chapters address some of the most basic concepts of estate planning, while the latter address the most complex. Hopefully, the confidence gained while reading the earlier Chapters will encourage you to tackle the more difficult material. Chapter 17 on retirement plan distributions is intimidating but is of critical importance. By retirement age, our retirement savings will likely be our largest single asset – contrary to the old motor oil commercials chiming that after your home, your *car* is likely your second most valuable asset! If I can motivate you to explore topics you had previously thought to be beyond your comprehension, I will have done my job.

As the name implies, *The Michigan Estate Planning Guide*, focuses on estate planning for Michigan residents. The concepts introduced herein are based on Michigan law, and should not be relied on by non-Michigan residents. Although federal law largely drives estate planning in all fifty states, certain aspects vary dramatically from state to state. The law pertaining to cessation of life support systems, state inheritance tax, probate, and intestate succession differ depending on domicile of the patient or decedent.

With minor exception, I have specifically omitted any self-help or do-it-yourself documents. These items have not been excluded to perpetuate the need for lawyers, but to avoid the pitfalls of self-help. A sad, but somewhat humorous, example of why we shouldn't act as our own attorney is the case of Warren Berger, former Chief Justice of the United States Supreme Court. Late in life, and soon after this wife's death, Justice Berger prepared his own Will. Having used a simple Will to pass his estate to his children, Justice Berger's entire estate was required to pass through probate. Since probate proceedings are a matter of public record, we were able to obtain a copy of Justice Berger's Will from Arlington County (Virginia) Probate Court. From the probate files we learned that Justice Berger's net worth at death was approximately $1.8 million, that he left one-third of his estate to his daughter and two-thirds to his son. Justice Berger's failure to prepare a proper estate plan subjected his estate to the cost, delay, and loss of privacy that probate entails. Justice Berger's estate could have been handled privately had he and his wife prepared revocable living trusts while they were both able.

Like Justice Berger, our own Coleman Young exposed himself to the indignity of probate. Coleman Young was a fiercely independent and private man. If he didn't like a Chapter, he would simply bark "none of your damn business." Yet, by passing his assets through his Will, he exposed his most private affairs to probate and public scrutiny. In his Will, reproduced in part below and obtained from the Wayne County Probate Court, the late Mayor provides for his housekeeper, family members and the son he at one time denied to be his own. By holding his son's inheritance "in trust" he commits a further gaffe. Trust arrangements created in a Will are known as "testamentary trusts," which must pass through probate not just at the time of the decedent's death, but each and every year thereafter until by its terms it expires.

Traditionally, the law relating to estate tax and estate planning has been extremely stable. Although there have been predictable changes, the new laws, once enacted, have provided adequate guidance for us to plan our future. Unlike past tax acts, The Economic Growth and Tax Relief Reconciliation Act of 2001 ("EGTRRA") is filled with uncertainties, and has made planning much more difficult. EGTRRA was the first tax act of President George W. Bush. It was billed as the final dagger to the heart of the unnecessary and unfair "death tax." With budget surpluses predicted far into the future, the estate tax was deemed to be unfair and expendable. As seen in Chapter 12, the new law would gradually phase out the estate tax until its total repeal in the year 2010. The new law has two major problems: First, the Act – as a result of the "Byrd Amendment" – comes back from the dead in 2011 (a year after its supposed elimination); and second, dramatic changes in the U.S. economy and world politics since September 11, 2001 bring into Chapter the advisability of eliminating the estate tax.

There will likely be legislation in the next few years that postpones, modifies, or repeals EGTRRA. Unfortunately, it is impossible to predict the content and form of future legislation. In the meantime, the only prudent course is to anticipate that some form of estate tax will exist far into the future and to proceed accordingly.

I hope the *Michigan Estate Planning Guide* allows you to make good estate planning decisions for you and your family. Read it in good health.

BOOK 156 PAGE 96
#22779

LAST WILL AND TESTAMENT
OF
WARREN E. BURGER

I hereby make and declare the following to be my last will and testament.

1. My exeuctors will first pay all claims against my estate;

2. The remainder of my estate will be distributed as follows: one-third to my daughter, Margaret Elizabeth Burger Rose and two-thirds to my son, Wade A. Burger;

3. I designate and appoint as executors of this will, Wade A. Burger and J. Michael Luttig.

IN WITNESS WHEREOF, I have hereunto set my hand to this my Last Will and Testament this ___9th___ day of June, 1994.

Warren E. Burger
WARREN E. BURGER

We hereby certify that in our presence on the date written above WARREN E. BURGER signed the foregoing instrument and declared it to be his Last Will and Testament and that at this request in his presence and in the presence of each other we have signed our names below as witnesses.

[signature] residing at 120 'F' St, NW
Washington, DC

[signature] residing at 3041. Meetig St
~~FAIRFAX VA~~ Falls Church, VA

SWORN TO AND SUBSCRIBED BEFORE ME THIS 9th
DAY OF ___June___, 19 94   _Constance Y. Ferguson_
NOTARY PUBLIC

CONSTANCE Y. FERGUSON
Notary Public, District of Columbia
My Commission Expires January 31, 1999

LAST WILL AND TESTAMENT

OF

COLEMAN A. YOUNG

I, **COLEMAN A. YOUNG**, of the City of Detroit, County of Wayne, State of Michigan, being of full age, sound and disposing mind and memory, not acting under menace, duress, fraud or undue influence of any person whomsoever, and hereby intending to dispose of all property belonging to me at my death, of whatever kind and wherever situate, do hereby make, declare, publish and constitute this to be my Last Will and Testament, to wit:

ARTICLE I

Section I.   At the time of execution of this Will, I am an unmarried single man.

Section 2.   My children, for purposes of his Will, shall mean, include and be limited to **Coleman A. Young, Jr.**

*   *   *   *

ARTICLE IV

GUARDIAN OF THE ESTATE OF MY CHILD

If the mother of my child does not survive me, I appoint **Patti Bell**, of Detroit, Michigan, as Guardian of the estate of my minor child, and I appoint **Shaunn Moore**, as alternate or successor Guardian. I direct that only a nominal bond be required of either Guardian named.

*   *   *   *

Section 3. I then direct that my Personal Representative pay to **Mrs. Wolf**, my housekeeper, an amount equal to six (6) months of her salary. I then direct that my Personal Representative pay to **Patricia Morefield**, my secretary, an amount equal to six (6) months of her salary.

*   *   *   *

Section 4. I then direct that my Personal Representative pay to my son, **Coleman A. Young, Jr.**, 25% of the remainder of my estate in the event that my son, **Coleman A. Young, Jr.**, has reached the age of majority. In the event that my son has not reached the age of majority, then 25% of the remainder of my estate, my son's share of my estate, shall be paid to the Trustee of my Family Trust, as described in Article VIII and administered in accordance therewith. I then direct that my Personal Representative pay 25% of the remainder of my estate to **Barbara Parker** of Detroit, Michigan. I then direct my Personal Representative to pay the balance of my estate equally to my two surviving sisters, **Bernice Grier** and **Juanita Clark**. The share of any beneficiary, who shall predecease me, shall be reallocated to the remaining beneficiaries.

*   *   *   *

ARTICLE VIII

FAMILY TRUST

My Trustee is hereby directed and authorized to receive all property, whether real or personal, distributed to him, by my Personal Representative, pursuant to the provisions of this my Last Will and Testament, and administer same as follows:

a.   The amount received by the Trustee, for the benefit of my son, **Coleman A. Young, Jr.**, shall be placed in a separate account and invested pursuant to the authority granted herein. Distributions shall be made to my son, **Coleman A. Young, Jr.**, in an amount equal to 25% (percent) of this Trust, on his 18th birthday, 25% on his 20th birthday, 25% on his 22nd birthday, and 25% on his 24th birthday. Thereafter, my son, **Coleman A. Young, Jr.**, shall have no further claims against the Trustee nor any interest in this Family Trust.

*   *   *   *

Signed by me on  Nov. 22 1995.

COLEMAN A. YOUNG

Notes

Chapter 1

What is an estate plan?

No better place to start than from the beginning! Estate planning is the process of assessing one's lifetime and testamentary goals. Lifetime estate planning goals typically include providing for one's own care in the event of incapacity. Testamentary estate planning goals include when and how to distribute assets at death, as well as the avoidance of probate and the elimination of estate tax.

The product of the estate planning process is the creation of an estate plan. The typical estate plan – to the extent there is such a thing - includes three documents: A Will, a durable power of attorney (actually, two powers: one for general matters and one for health care – see Chapter 3), and a revocable living trust. Each of these documents allows for the appointment of trusted individuals (or sometimes institutions) known as "fiduciaries," to carry out the wishes of the maker at the time of death or incapacity. Ideally, an estate planning attorney works with the client and the client's financial advisor to identify the client's wishes and then recommends the documents and steps necessary to implement those wishes. Let's take a closer look at the fundamental building blocks of estate planning:

Last Will and Testament

A Personal Representative (formerly known as "Executor" or "Executrix") is nominated by the decedent in his or her Last Will and Testament ("Will") to make funeral arrangements, disburse personal property, and if necessary, to represent the estate in probate court. The Guardian of minor children is also typically appointed in the Will. A Will used in conjunction with a revocable living trust is known as a "pour over Will" and serves as a safety net to transfer probatable assets (i.e. assets which were not transferred into trust during life) into trust at death. A Will comes into effect only upon the testator's death (see Chapter 4).

Durable Power of Attorney

A durable power of attorney allows the maker to appoint an agent to manage his or her personal affairs, and a "patient advocate" to make medical decisions in the event the maker becomes incompetent. Common practice is to employ two separate durable powers of attorney, one for health care (Durable Power of Attorney for Health Care) and a second for general matters (General Durable Power of Attorney). Since 1991, Michigan law – in line with the other 49 states – allows for the appointment of a patient advocate to withdraw life support systems in the event of terminal illness. Depending on its terms, a durable power of attorney comes into effect either on the date signed or upon the total incapacity of its maker (a "springing" power), and in all cases ends on the maker's death (see Chapter 3). "Living wills" are not recognized in Michigan.

Revocable Living Trust

The revocable living trust is perhaps the most important and versatile estate planning tool. It operates to avoid probate, provide for children of the current or prior marriage, minimize federal estate tax and accomplish a whole host of other estate planning objectives. A revocable living trust is effective upon execution and continues to be effective after the death of its maker (called the "Grantor"). Assets passing through a revocable living trust avoid probate since the death of the Grantor does not affect the continued existence of the trust.

Although, for some, revocable living trusts may seem like a new concept, they have actually been around for centuries. The current popularity of revocable trusts is due to a number of factors including media attention, the changing American family, and inflation.

The increasing number of families with children from previous marriages has also added to the growth of revocable living trusts. It is only through the use of revocable living trusts that a parent can properly provide for his or her children not of the current marriage. For example, a revocable living trust can be designed to provide support to a second wife after the husband's death, with the balance of the trust assets remaining at the death of the second wife being distributed to the husband's children from his first marriage (see Chapter 13). Without the use of trusts, assets would simply pass outright to the wife with no guarantee that the husband's children would receive an inheritance.

Revocable living trusts can be used to preserve each spouse's Applicable Exclusion Amount, resulting in significant estate tax savings. Every person may leave up to $1,000,000[1] (2002-2003) to his or her beneficiaries without the imposition of federal estate tax. Although this may seem like a very large figure, inflation, growth in the stock market and the popularity of individual account balance retirement plans such as 401(k) plans place an ever-increasing number of Americans in a taxable position. Revocable living trusts help solve this problem by allowing married couples to leave up to $2 million dollars to the next generation estate tax free (2002-2003). (See Chapter 12).

While the Grantor is alive, revocable trusts are not subject to income tax and thus do not file annual income tax returns.[2] By retaining the power to amend, revoke and otherwise control the trust, the Grantor of a revocable trust reports all trust income on his or her personal income tax return. Assets owned in trust continue to use the social security number of the Grantor as their tax identifier.

Recent Michigan legislation has increased the attractiveness of trusts by according them the same protection from creditors previously afforded only to assets passing through probate. Under the Estates and Protected Individuals Code ("EPIC"),[3] Successor Trustees (i.e., the trustee who takes over for the Grantor/trustee at the Grantor's death) are permitted to identify and pay claims in much the same way as estates subject to probate (see Chapter 7). Trusts are now required to publish notice of the death of the Grantor. The effect of the new notice procedure is to effectively shorten the statute of limitations on claims against a trust from six years to only four months. As with probate proceedings, the claims of creditors who fail to make a claim within the four-month publication period are barred.

A number of more sophisticated estate planning concepts and strategies can be employed by larger estates to minimize or avoid estate tax. These concepts are discussed in the chapters that follow, and include discussion of irrevocable trusts (Chapter15), Limited Liability Companies (Chapter16) and Charitable Trusts (Chapter18).

Miscellaneous Documents

Other ancillary documents are used in estate planning: a "Letter of Instruction" identifies immediate steps to be taken at the time of death including instructions relating to final arrangements, funeral wishes, and cremation; and a "Personal Property Memorandum," indicates the individuals who are to inherit particular items of personal property such as jewelry, collectibles and other family heirlooms (see example on page 28). Anatomical gifts should also be addressed in the estate planning process. Other important documents, such as a company buy-sell agreement, may need to be reviewed to ensure that they are consistent with the client's estate planning objectives.

How to Get Started

Choose Fiduciaries. As with any important decision, the best place to start is by putting your thoughts down on paper. Start by identifying the people you want to act on your behalf in the event of your death or incapacity. A fiduciary is a person or entity appointed to act on another's behalf. Fiduciaries are held to a high standard of care to act solely for the benefit of the person who has appointed them, and not for their own benefit. Certainly, if you're going to make the effort to plan your estate, you want to be assured that your wishes will be carried out. Make sure that your fiduciaries are competent to act, understand your wishes and are likely to carry them out. The three most difficult jobs to fill tend to be the guardian of minor children, the patient advocate charged with making medical decisions and the successor trustee appointed to manage trust assets after the death of grantor and grantor's spouse (if married). After making these tough decisions, it is advisable to choose alternates to act in the event your first choice is unable or unwilling to act.

Name Beneficiaries. Who is to inherit your estate? Only in extremely rare circumstances should you leave your estate to your children any way other than equally. Unequal shares leave a legacy of hurt feelings and estrangement between or among your children. Naturally, the distribution pattern is much more complex where a couple has children from prior marriages. The "mine, yours, and ours" syndrome of the modern family is quite real when you consider that nearly one-half of the marriages in this country end in divorce, and at least half of all divorced people marry again. Balancing among the needs and expectations of children from different marriages and the needs of the surviving spouse is a complex undertaking that requires mature and candid discussions between the couple and an informed and intuitive professional advisor. See Chapter13 for a discussion of the special considerations that apply to second marriages.

Control from the Grave. Controlling from the grave isn't necessarily a bad thing. Younger beneficiaries shouldn't inherit too early. Certainly, eighteen year old children cannot be permitted unfettered control of their inheritance, nor should beneficiaries with emotional or substance abuse problems or beneficiaries with an acute allergy to work. One clever client, who placed a high value on hard work and self-reliance, directed that no child, no matter what age, should inherit an amount in any year that exceeded the beneficiary's earned (W2) income. In the client's view, an inheritance should reward hard work, not take the place of it.

The job of the estate planning attorney is to apply the law to accomplish the objectives of the client. Ideally, probate is avoided, estate tax is eliminated, the surviving spouse continues to live the life to which he or she became accustomed during the life of both spouses, and the children of the marriage (or previous marriages) are properly remembered.

An estate planning questionnaire is attached as Exhibit C. The questionnaire isn't just for the benefit of the estate planning attorney; it should also aid the client in organizing his or her thoughts. There are a number of chapters aimed at assessing the net worth of the client for estate tax purposes. From the author's experience, most clients are surprised to learn the size of their estate. The questionnaire asks the client to assess the relative physical and mental health of children. Completing an estate planning questionnaire prior to the first meeting with the estate planning attorney can be a good way to provoke thought and to open the lines of communication between the client and the attorney.

Notes

Chapter 2

What assets are included in a decedent's estate?

In large part, the size of an estate dictates the estate planning documents and strategies to be employed. Accordingly, initial estate planning discussions soon turn to the client's assets. The starting point is to determine the client's "gross estate". Basically, the gross estate is the total value of the client's assets. Certain deductions are then allowed in determining the "adjusted gross estate." Further deductions reduce the adjusted gross estate to arrive at the taxable estate. The diagram that follows illustrates the circuitous journey from the gross estate to the estate tax due. It also provides an overview of a number of the topics discussed later in the book.

Gross Estate[4]
    (Funeral and Administrative)*
    (indebtedness and taxes)
    (losses)

Adjusted Gross Estate
    (Marital Deduction) see Chapter 10
    (Charitable deductions) see Chapter 18

Taxable Estate[5]
    x (times) Tax rate %

Tentative Tax
(Unified Credit) see Chapter 12
(State death tax credit)

Estate tax due
* Parentheses indicate subtraction

The term "gross estate" includes all property in which the decedent had a beneficial interest at the time of death.[6] The most obvious examples are cash, stocks, bonds, real estate, business interests, artwork and other personal tangible property. The following is a more complete list of assets included in the gross estate listed by category:

Tangible
- Cash
- Cars and other vehicles (including boats and recreation vehicles)
- Precious metals, jewelry and furs
- Antiques, collectibles and works of art
- Household goods, clothing and other miscellaneous personal property

Intangible
- Savings and Checking accounts
- Money Market and Certificates of Deposit
- Stocks and bonds
- Mutual Funds
- Vested interest in profit sharing plan, stock options, 401(k) and IRA Plans
- Life Insurance
- Trademarks and royalties. Interests in LLCs, partnerships, sole proprietorships and corporations
- Miscellaneous receivables (mortgages, promissory notes, rents due)

Real Estate
- Homes, condominiums, time shares, business and investment properties, as well as undeveloped and agricultural land.

The gross estate includes other complex ownership interests over which the decedent retains the requisite control. The balance of this Chapter 2 addresses the question of what is included in the gross estate. Many of the rules of inclusion deviate from standard financial and accounting principals, while some appear to have no basis in logic.

Life Insurance

The full *face* value of life insurance is included in the decedent's gross estate if the decedent maintained any "incidents of ownership" over the policy.[7] Incidents of ownership are ownership-type rights, such as the right to change the beneficiary or borrow from the policy.

The increased life expectancy of Americans has resulted in lower life insurance premium costs and substantially larger face values. Large life insurance proceeds – although extremely beneficial the decedent's family – can inflate the value of an estate, causing unexpected estate tax consequences. To avoid estate tax, it may be advisable to own life insurance in an irrevocable trust (see Chapter 15). A properly drafted irrevocable trust separates the incidents of ownership from the decedent, thereby excluding the proceeds from the decedent's estate.

Retirement Plan Assets

The full value of IRA, 401(k) and other retirement plan account balances is included in the decedent's estate.[8] Distributions from these plans are *also* subject to income tax.[9] The possibility of double taxation on retirement type assets requires special planning (see Chapter 17). With proper planning, IRA distributions may be "stretched" over the life expectancy of the surviving spouse and the children of the decedent, thereby dramatically postponing the income tax on such distributions.

Jointly held Assets

One-half (1/2) of the value of assets owned jointly with a spouse are included in the gross estate of a decedent.[10] One hundred (100%) percent of assets held jointly with a non-spouse are included in the decedent's estate where the decedent supplied all of the original consideration.[11] For example, the entire value of a joint savings account would be included in mom's estate where mom simply added her son's name to the account for sake of convenience or to avoid probate. Clients often mistakenly believe that they are making gifts by adding their children's names to their assets, when in reality the asset is fully included in the decedent's estate. Assets held jointly with a spouse receive a stepped up basis as to one-half of the date-of-death value of the asset. As a consolation prize, assets held jointly with a non-spouse, which are fully included in the decedent's estate, receive a full stepped-up basis for income tax purposes.[12] See Chapter 11 for a discussion of the stepped up basis and new (post 2001 Act) "carry-over" basis rules.

Gifts of the following types of property must be brought back into the decedent's gross estate: (1) gifts of property in which the decedent retained a life estate; (2) certain gifts of property that only vest if the donee survives decedent; (3) gifts subject to revocation by the decedent; and (4) gifts of life insurance policies insuring the decedent's life if made within three years of death.[13]

Transfers with a Retained Life Estate

The gross estate includes the value of any property that the decedent transfers if he or she retains the right to possession or enjoyment of the property, or the right to income from that property. For example, if the decedent transfers his home to his child, but retains the right to live in the home during his life, the entire date of death value of the home will be included in the gross estate.[14]

Revocable Transfers

If a decedent made a transfer of property during his lifetime, but retained the power to alter, amend, revoke or terminate the enjoyment of the property at any time up to and including the date of death, the value of the property is included in the decedent's gross estate.[15] Consequently, the entire value of a revocable living trust is included in the grantor's estate.

Powers of Appointment

The gross estate includes the value of property over which the decedent has a general power of appointment.[16] A general power of appointment is a power given to the decedent by a third party to consume, invade or appropriate the property in favor of the decedent, his estate or his creditors. If the power is a lifetime power and is limited by an "ascertainable standard" relating to the health, education, support, or maintenance of the decedent, then the power is deemed not to be a "general power of appointment" for estate tax purposes. The most common power of appointment is found in marital trusts (see Chapter 10). A marital trust power of appointment allows the surviving spouse to appoint the balance of the marital trust remaining at her death to a beneficiary of the surviving spouse's choosing. As a result, the entire value of the marital trust (valued as of the date of the surviving spouse's death) is included in the surviving spouse's estate.

Valuation

Assets are included in the gross estate at their fair market value as of the date of the decedent's death. Special valuation rules are available for certain special use assets such as business property and farmland.[17] The "alternate valuation date" (the date six months following the date of death of the decedent) may be elected where the value of the decedent's estate declined during the six-month period following the decedent's death[18] (see Chapter 11). Naturally, the fair market value of cash and traded securities can be determined from the newspaper. An independent appraiser must value real estate and business interests. Obtaining the proper appraised value of property is necessary to avoid later conflict with the IRS, and for purposes of establishing the stepped-up basis of the asset.

Chapter 3

Are durable powers of attorney included in most estate plans?

Yes, durable powers of attorney are a standard and integral component of most estate plans. Durable powers of attorney allow their maker to appoint another individual (an "agent" in a General Durable Power of Attorney, and a "Patient Advocate" in a Durable Power of Attorney for Health Care) to act on their behalf. Essentially, the maker of a power of attorney can delegate to another any power he or she possesses personally.

The term "durable" signifies that the power being granted continues to be effective despite the disability of the maker. Since the likelihood of becoming incompetent increase dramatically as we age, it is important that we appoint trusted family members or friends to handle our affairs in the event that we are unable to act on our own behalf. Absent proper planning, the affairs of an incompetent come within the jurisdiction of the probate court. A family member or other "interested party" would be required to petition the probate court to have the individual declared incompetent, and to have a guardian and conservator appointed. Durable powers of attorney (DPOA) have become essential estate planning components primarily due to their efficacy in avoiding costly and time-consuming probate court proceedings.

Durable powers of attorney can be broken into two broad categories: General durable powers and durable powers for health care.0

General Durable Powers of Attorney

Under a general durable power of attorney (DPOA), the maker appoints an agent to handle all of his or her personal business, including banking, preparation and filing of tax returns, sale of motor vehicles, application for

Social Security and governmental benefits, all as if the maker were himself or herself present. Depending on the level of trust the maker has in his or her agent, a DPOA can be effective either as of its execution or upon the maker's disability (a "springing power"). Naturally, there is a much greater potential for misuse where the DPOA is effective upon signing. For this reason, the author typically recommends springing DPOAs.

A DPOA grants to the agent the power to handle asll of the maker's *personal* affairs. The power of the agent does *not* extend to assets owned by the maker's revocable living trust. Assets owned by the maker's revocable living trust are not considered the maker's personal assets. The revocable living trust itself addresses the issue of the disability by appointing a successor trustee upon the disability of the grantor/initial trustee.

Under Michigan law, an agent may not make gifts without specific authorization in the document.[19] It is important to grant the agent the power to make gifts in cases where the maker has commenced an annual gifting program for the purpose of reducing his or her taxable estate (see Chapter16). Absent the specific power to gift, the gifting program would be stalled by the disability of the donor. The power to gift may be especially important if a gifting program has been initiated for Medicaid planning purposes. A gifting program can be designed to reduce the patients "countable" assets without disqualifying him or her for Medicaid benefits. To maximize the amount that can be legally divested, it is important that the gifting program continue after the disability of the patient. A durable power of attorney that grants the power to gift assures that the gifting program can continue after such disability (see Chapter 19).

Durable Powers for Health Care

Advances in medical science have created a health care dilemma: how long to keep terminally ill patients alive on life support systems? Fortunately, in late 1990, Michigan law was changed to allow for the appointment of a substituted decision maker in cases where the patient is unable to make his or her own medical decisions (mandatory springing power).[20] Michigan law now recognizes health care powers of attorney ("HCPOA"), which designate a "patient advocate" to make an individual's health care decisions. The patient advocate may be given the authority to pull the plug in the event of terminal illness. Under Michigan law, the authority of the patient advocate comes into effect only when the patient is unable to participate in his or her own medical treatment decisions. To preserve the patient's right to self-determination, the law reserves unto the patient the power to make his or her own medical decisions as long as he or she is able. The determination of the patient's ability to participate in medical decisions is to be made by the patient's "attending physician or another physician or licensed psychologist."[21] The patient advocate has the legal authority to work directly with the patient's doctors to determine the nature and extent of the patient's medical treatment, including decisions relating to life support system cessation. Absent a properly drafted HCPOA, the legal authority to make an incompetent patient's medical decisions can be granted only with probate court intervention. "Living Wills" and other informal documents are not effective for the purposes of making health care designations.

To be effective, a HCPOA must be signed in the presence of two witnesses, neither of whom are the patient's spouse, parent, child, grandchild, sibling, heir, physician, patient advocate, or an employee of a life or health insurance provider, health facility, or a home for the aged. The HCPOA must be dated, and must contain specific language exonerating health care professionals from liability for terminating life support systems. It must also clearly state that the patient understands that a decision of the patient advocate "could or would lead to my death." All patient advocates must sign an "Acceptance of Patient Advocate" form, agreeing to act on behalf of the patient in conformity with Michigan law. Perhaps most important of all, a HCPOA must be signed when the patient is competent.

HCPOAs executed prior to 1991 are grandfathered from the technical requirements of the 1990 law. However, pre-1991 HCPOAs should be revoked and replaced with a HCPOA valid under current law for the reason that physicians and hospital medical ethics boards will be very reluctant to honor HCPOAs that do not contain current language. Also, HCPOAs should be reviewed and re-executed from time to time. Even valid HCPOAs can become "stale" if many years have passed since their execution, bringing into question whether they have been revoked or revised in the intervening period. Although there is no legislatively mandated limit on validity for Michigan HCPOAs – unlike several other States which dictate how long a HCPOA will be effective – it is the author's view that HCPOAs should be revised and updated every five to seven years.

Since it is impossible to specifically address every medi-cal contingency in a HCPOA, HCPOAs tend to grant the patient advocate wide discretion. It is therefore important to choose a patient advocate who understands your wishes, especially with respect to continued life support. For this reason, spouses, parents and adult children with whom the maker has a trusting relationship are the most logical choices to act as patient advocate. The author recommends empowering only one patient advocate at a time; naming multiple patient advocates with concurrent power only creates the possibility for conflict. A successor patient advocate should be named in the event that the patient's first choice is unable or unwilling to act. Hospitals cannot be expected to terminate life support systems when they receive conflicting instructions from concurrent or multiple patient advocates.

The detailed health care directive below outlines a number of illnesses and the corresponding level of intervention desired by the patient. Although the author in his estate planning practice does not use this form, the reader may benefit from the detail provided by the form. If nothing else, the form should provoke some thought.

Recent studies have confirmed what the general public had long suspected. Health care directives, even when in writing and communicated to the physician, are often ignored by hospitals.[22] For this reason, patients must be diligent in every aspect of their HCPOA. Patients must verbally communicate their thoughts and wishes concerning terminal illness and life support systems to their patient advocate. The treating physician and hospital should be aware that a HCPOA has been prepared, and should be given a copy of the document. Knowing of the reluctance of hospitals and physicians to remove patients from life support systems, the patient or the patient advocate will have to be assertive and vigilant. If the health care facility fails to respond appropriately, you may find it useful to have a hospice organization intervene on your behalf. It's your right!

The federal Patient Self Determination Act requires all Medicare-eligible health care facilities to inform patients of their rights regarding health care decision-making. So, don't be surprised during the admissions process when you are asked if you have a HCPOA. The bar associations of most states – including Michigan – have drafted sample health care directive forms that can be used in emergency situations where the patient is competent at the time of admission. Despite the fact that all fifty states recognize the right of the individual to appoint a health care advocate and to terminate life support systems under certain circumstances, the laws of the states differ substantially. Health care powers of attorney executed in one state are not necessarily enforceable in other states. Therefore, separate HCPOAs should be drafted for individuals splitting time between or among states.

Durable powers of attorney may be revoked as long as the maker is competent. The best way to revoke DPOAs or HCPOA is to destroy all copies of the document.

Agents and patient advocates are "fiduciaries" under Michigan law. As such, they are held to a high ethical standard to act in the best interest of the person granting the power. Breach of a fiduciary duty or standard of care exposes the fiduciary to civil – and in rare cases criminal – liability. Appointing a fiduciary, or being asked to act as one, is a serious matter that requires a great deal of aforethought. It is prudent to discuss the appointment with your friend or family member prior to completing the necessary documents.

Michigan passed the "Do-Not-Resuscitate Act" to protect terminally ill patients. The product of the legislation is the "Do-Not-Resuscitate Order," which legally prohibits EMS units and other emergency caregivers from resuscitating the terminally ill homebound patient. See Exhibit "A" for an example of the Do-Not-Resuscitate Order.

MY MEDICAL DIRECTIVE*

This Medical Directive expresses, and shall stand for, my wishes regarding medical treatments in the event that illness should make me unable to communicate them directly. I make this Directive, being 18 years or more of age, of sound mind and appreciating the consequences of my decisions.

SITUATION (A)

If I am in a coma or in a persistent vegetative state, and in the opinion of my physician and several consultants have no known hope of regaining awareness and higher mental functions no matter what is done, then my wishes regarding use of the following, if considered medically reasonable, would be:

☐ prolong life; treat everything
☐ attempt to cure, but reevaluate often
☐ limit to less invasive and less
   burdonsome interventions
☐ provide comfort care only
☐ other (please specify): _____

_____

	I want	Do not want	I am undecided	I want treatment tried. If no clear improvement, stop.
1. CARDIOPULMONARY RESUSCITATION (chest compressions, drugs, electric shocks, and artificial breathing aimed at reviving a person who is on the point of dying).				Not applicable
2. MECHANICAL BREATHING (respiration by machine, through a tube in the throat).				
3. ARTIFICIAL NUTRITION AND HYDRATION (given through a tube in a vein or in the stomach).				
4. MAJOR SURGERY (for example, removing the gall bladder or part of the colon).				Not applicable
5. DIALYSIS (cleaning the blood by machine or by fluid passed through the belly).				
6. BLOOD TRANSFUSIONS OR BLOOD PRODUCTS				Not applicable
7. ANTIBIOTICS (drugs to fight infection).				Not applicable
8. SIMPLE DIAGNOSTIC TESTS (for example, blood tests or x-rays).				Not applicable
9. PAIN MEDICATION (even if they dull consciousness and indirectly shorten my life				Not applicable

* Printed with permission of Linda and Zeke Emmanuel of Emmanuel and Emmanuel, Chicago, Illinois.

SITUATION (B)

If I am in a coma and I have a small likelihood of recovering fully, a slightly larger likelihood of surviving with permanent brain damage, and a much larger likelihood of dying, then my wishes regarding the use of the following, if considered medically reasonable, would be:

- [ ] prolong life; treat everything
- [ ] attempt to cure, but reevaluate often
- [ ] limit to less invasive and less burdonsome interventions
- [ ] provide comfort care only
- [ ] other (please specify): _____

SITUATION (C)

If I have brain damage or some brain disease which cannot be reversed and which makes me unable to recognize people, or to speak understandably, and I also have a terminal illness, such as incurable cancer which will likely be the cause of my death, then my wishes regarding use of the following, if considered medically reasonable, would be:

- [ ] prolong life; treat everything
- [ ] attempt to cure, but reevaluate often
- [ ] limit to less invasive and less burdonsome interventions
- [ ] provide comfort care only
- [ ] other (please specify): _____

SITUATION (D)

If I have brain damage or some brain disease which cannot be reversed and which makes me unable to recognize people, or to speak understandably, but I have no terminal illness, and I can live in this condition for a long time, then my wishes regarding use of the ollowing, if considered medically reasonable, would be:

- [ ] prolong life; treat everything
- [ ] attempt to cure, but reevaluate often
- [ ] limit to less invasive and less burdonsome interventions
- [ ] provide comfort care only
- [ ] other (please specify): _____

I want	Do not want	I am undecided	I want treatment tried. If no clear improvement, stop.		I want	Do not want	I am undecided	I want treatment tried. If no clear improvement, stop.		I want	Do not want	I am undecided	I want treatment tried. If no clear improvement, stop.
			Not applicable					Not applicable					Not applicable
			Not applicable					Not applicable					Not applicable
			Not applicable					Not applicable					Not applicable
			Not applicable					Not applicable					Not applicable
			Not applicable					Not applicable					Not applicable
			Not applicable					Not applicable					Not applicable

SITUATION (E)

If I (describe situation that is important to you and/or your doctor believes you should consider in view of your current medical situation):

- prolong life; treat everything
- attempt to cure, but reevaluate often
- limit to less invasive and less burdonsome interventions
- provide comfort care only
- other (please specify): _____

_____

SITUATION (F)

If I am in my current state of health (describe briefly): _____

_____

and then have an illness that, in the opinion of my physician and two consultants, is life threatening but reversible, and I am temporarily unable to make decisions, then my goals and specific wishes – if medically reasonable – would be:

- prolong life; treat everything
- attempt to cure, but reevaluate often
- limit to less invasive and less burdonsome interventions
- provide comfort care only
- other (please specify): _____

_____

I want	Do not want	I am undecided	I want treatment tried. If no clear improvement, stop.
			Not applicable
			Not applicable
			Not applicable
			Not applicable
			Not applicable
			Not applicable

I want	Do not want	I am undecided	I want treatment tried. If no clear improvement, stop.
			Not applicable
			Not applicable
			Not applicable
			Not applicable
			Not applicable
			Not applicable

Chapter 4

Is a will still necessary if you have a revocable living trust?

The short answer is "Yes." A Will performs a number of essential functions not addressed in other estate planning documents. In a Will, the testator appoints his or her personal representative, the guardian and conservator of minor children, disposes of personal property, and in the case of individuals who have revocable living trusts, "pours over" assets at death which were not transferred into trust during life.

Personal Representative

The personal representative ("PR") is the modern day Executor/Executrix. The terminology has changed somewhat over the years, but the job of the PR has essentially stayed the same. The PR makes the decedent's funeral arrangements, distributes personal property (i.e., jewelry, furniture, automobiles, etc.) to the named beneficiaries, and represents the estate in matters of probate. Ideally, the decedent has created a revocable living trust and has re-titled all of his or her assets into the trust to avoid probate. The Will acts as a safety net to catch any asset that the decedent failed to transfer to trust during his or her lifetime, and "pours" such assets over to the trust (thus the name "Pour Over Will"). Unfortunately, assets poured into the trust through the Will must pass through probate. Once in the trust, the assets will be held and administered according to the terms of the trust.

Personal Effects Memorandum

Rather than itemize and distribute personal property in the Will document, it has become the legal custom to refer to a "separate writing" which details the disposition of tangible personal property. In the separate writing, the testator lists heirloom items and names the beneficiary to receive each item. Since the personal effects memorandum is separate and apart from the Will, it may be amended without amending the Will and without incurring legal fees. This approach has gained popularity since it is not economical to amend a Will to alter something as minor as a change of heart concerning personal property. A Will amendment is known as a "codicil."

PERSONAL EFFECTS MEMORANDUM

I, Wendy Barnes, hereby make this Personal Effects Memorandum pursuant to paragraph SECOND (d) of my Last Will and Testament dated September 1, 2003.

I give and bequeath the following property as specified:

1. My 14 karat gold bracelet with three diamonds to my son, Sam Barnes.

2. A pair of 10 karat gold earrings (hoops) to my daughter, Donna Barnes.

3. My Roman Coin pendant necklace to my nephew, Neil Smith.

4. My 14 karat gold necklace (chain-link) to my niece, Norma Smith.

Dated: September 1, 2003

Wendy Barnes
WENDY BARNES

Guardian and Conservator

The guardian and conservator of minor children are typically named in the Will. To cover unforeseen contingencies, a primary and alternate guardian should be appointed. It is recommended that prospective guardians be contacted to confirm that they are willing to take on the responsibility of acting as guardian. The sobering responsibility of raising children makes appointing a guardian one of the most difficult – and frequently amended – estate planning decisions.

The guardian has legal authority over the *person* of the minor child, while the conservator manages the *financial affairs* of the minor child. The job of a conservator is much less important when the client has a revocable living trust; since the successor trustee under the trust manages all trust assets on behalf of the minor.

Where parents of minor children are divorced, the custodial parent would often prefer to name a guardian other than the non-custodial spouse. Although the custodial parent may name a third party guardian, the election will likely not be honored if the non-custodial parent objects. Michigan's Child Custody Act creates a strong preference for the biological non-custodial parent to take over the custodial responsibilities of a minor child upon the death of the custodial parent. Nonetheless, the custodial parent should select a third party guardian on the outside chance that the non-custodial parent may predecease the custodial parent, or is unable or unwilling to take over the legal responsibilities of raising the minor child.

Testamentary Trusts

In those rare cases where a trust is not utilized, a "Simple" Will is used to distribute assets at death. Assets passing through a Will of any kind, including a Simple Will, pass through probate.

Testamentary Trusts are trusts that come into being upon the death of the testator (unlike revocable living trusts which are effective upon signing). Typically, Testamentary Trust provisions are added to a Will (sometimes called a "Will with Testamentary Trust"). Testamentary Trusts are disfavored since they require full probate supervision upon the death of the testator.

Capacity

Any person eighteen years or older who is of sound mind can execute a Will.[23] To be valid in Michigan, a Will must be witnessed by at least two persons. The witnesses should not be related to the testator, and should not be a named beneficiary under the Will. A "self-proving" Will creates the presumption that it was properly executed by the decedent. To be self-proving the witnesses must acknowledge in writing that they witnessed the testator sign the Will voluntarily, and that to the best of their knowledge the testator is at least eighteen years of age, of sound mind, and under no constraint or undue influence. An un-witnessed Will may nonetheless be honored if it qualifies as a "holographic" Will under Michigan law.[24]

Intestacy

Someone dying without a Will is said to have died "intestate." If a person dies without a Will, the Michigan statutes of descent and distribution[25] determine who receives the decedent's probatable assets (see Chapter 5).

Chapter 5

What happens if I die without a will?

If you die without a Will, you are said to have died "intestate." Contrary to popular myth, if you die without a Will your property does not pass to the State of Michigan. Instead, your property subject to probate is distributed according to the State of Michigan's rules of intestate succession. The intestate succession laws assign default beneficiaries based on what the legislature believes to be the wishes of the average person. Naturally, had the decedent drafted a valid Will or trust when the decedent was competent, his exact wishes would have been given effect. Absent such direction, the legislature was forced to create a method of descent and distribution that would approximate the wishes of the average Michigan resident. What the legislature created, as it is more fully described below, is a system that favors one's surviving spouse and children, followed by more distant relatives. Only when no immediate relatives exist does the State of Michigan become the beneficiary. In such circumstances, the decedent's estate is said to "escheat" to the state.

A probate proceeding must be commenced in the county of the decedent's domicile in order to: 1) appoint the decedent's Personal Representative; and, 2) determine the rightful beneficiaries of the decedent's assets subject to probate. *Jointly owned assets and assets that name a beneficiary do not pass through probate, and accordingly are not governed by the laws of intestate succession.* Instead, such assets pass by operation of law to the joint owner or named beneficiary. Only assets owned solely in the decedent's name pass through probate and are subject to the intestate succession rules described on the following page.

Decedents dying without a Will are subject to the following distribution scheme (as revised by the Estates and Protected Individuals Code ("EPIC")):

If you are survived by a spouse and children of that marriage,

    A. $165,000 and 1/2 of the balance of your estate goes to your spouse;[26]

    B. The rest of your estate is equally divided among your children;[27]

    C. The children of a deceased child take their parent's share, except that if more than one of your children predeceased you with children of their own, all of your surviving grandchildren will take equal shares of your estate.[28]

If you are survived by a spouse and children *not* of that marriage (i.e., if you have children from a prior marriage who survive you),

    A. $110,000 and 1/2 of the balance of your estate goes to your spouse;[29]

    B. The rest of your estate is equally divided among your children;

If you are survived by a spouse, but have no children,

    A. $165,000 and 3/4 of the balance of your estate goes to your spouse;[30]

    B. The rest of your estate passes to your parents (or the survivor).[31]

If you are survived by a spouse, but no children or parents,

    A. All of your property passes to your spouse.[32]

    B. All dollar figures are annually indexed for inflation.[33] Also, no distinction is made based on gender of the surviving spouse.

If you die with no surviving spouse, but with children (or their descendants),

    A. Your estate is divided equally among your children;[34]

    B. The children of a deceased child take their parent's share, except that if more than one of your children predecease you and both had children, all of your surviving grandchildren will take equal shares of your estate.[35]

If you die with no surviving spouse and no children,

    A. Your entire estate passes to your parents (or the survivor);[36]

    B. If neither parent survives you, your estate goes to your brothers and sisters in equal shares.[37]

    C. The children of a deceased sibling take their parent's share, except that if more than one of your siblings predecease you and both had children, all of your surviving nieces and nephews will take equal shares of your estate.[38]

If you die without a surviving spouse, children, parents, brothers, sisters, or children of brothers or sisters,

    A. One-half of your estate passes to your paternal grandparents or their descendants) and one-half passes to your maternal grandparents (or their descendants). Under EPIC, the pool of beneficiaries in this situation includes children of predeceased nieces and nephews, if you have no surviving children, parents or siblings.[39]

If you die without any relatives who survive you,

    A. All of your estate passes to the State of Michigan.

Obviously, the preferred approach is to thoughtfully name your fiduciaries and beneficiaries rather than rely on the Michigan one-size-fits-all rules of intestate succession. See Chapter 7 for a more complete discussion of the probate process.

Notes

Chapter 6

Do jointly held assests and property that names a beneficiary avoid probate?

Yes, both jointly held assets and assets that name a beneficiary avoid probate. Jointly held assets pass from the deceased joint tenant to the surviving tenant by operation of law and therefore are not subject to probate.[40] Typical forms of joint tenancy include "joint tenants with rights of survivorship" (sometimes referred to as "JTWROS"),[41] and, if between spouses, "tenancy by the entireties."[42] Other methods of transfer, like transfer on death ("TOD") or pay on death ("POD") designations,[43] and beneficiary designations, also pass by operation of law and avoid probate.

Although jointly held property avoids probate, there are a number of reasons not to use joint ownership as a form of estate planning. On the other hand, beneficiary and TOD designations can be essential estate planning tools if used properly.

Joint Tenancy

No question, a great many married couples own some or all of their assets jointly. At the first spouse's death, the couple's jointly held assets pass automatically to the surviving spouse. Thus, transition at the time of the first spouse's death is relatively easy for such couples. However, the Applicable Exclusion Amount of the deceased spouse has been permanently lost. For couples with estates in excess of the Applicable Exclusion Amount ($1,000,000 in 2002-2003), it is critical that all joint tenancies be severed to permit assets to be transferred ("funded") to each spouse's *separate* revocable living trust. Spouses are often reluctant to dissolve their joint tenancies until they learn of the tremendous estate tax benefits in doing so.

There is an unavoidable loss of control that occurs when additional tenants (owners) are added to an asset. Adding tenants exposes the asset to the claims of the creditors of the new joint tenants.[44] Joint ownership is not usually a problem between spouses, however, adding children or other family members as co-owners after the death of a spouse can result in loss of control, liability exposure, and inequitable bequests.

Adding a child as joint tenant on an asset accords significant lifetime rights to the child and significantly diminishes the parent's rights with respect to the control and disposition of the asset. For example, if mom adds her children as joint tenants on her home, she cannot sell or mortgage her home without the consent of her children. What's worse, if she has boys, their wives obtain a dower interest in mom's home and must therefore consent to any sale or mortgage as well. Even if the children consent to the mortgage or sale of the home, they would technically be entitled to their share of the proceeds from the sale, a result mom certainly didn't intend. Further, in the event of divorce of one of the children, a son-in-law or daughter-in-law may claim a spousal interest in the home.

There is no guarantee that the intended beneficiary will actually receive the jointly held asset. Typically, parents wish to leave their assets equally to their children, with the share of a deceased child passing to the children of such predeceased child. This objective cannot be achieved by titling assets jointly. Under joint ownership, only the surviving named beneficiaries have an ownership interest. Thus, if mom adds her three children as joint tenants on her home and bank accounts, and one her children predeceases her, only the *two* surviving children inherit, leaving the children of the deceased child out in the cold.

Transfer on Death

In late 1996, Michigan joined the vast majority of states in adopting the Uniform Transfer-on-Death Security Registration Act.[45] Prior to passage of the Act, securities such as stocks, bonds and mutual funds, would not allow for the designation of a beneficiary. The legislation enables individual or joint account owners to name beneficiaries to receive their securities upon their death rather than through a probated distribution. To be registered in beneficiary form, the account must use the designation "pay on death" ("POD") or "transfer on death" ("TOD"). If there are multiple account *owners* (for example a husband and wife), the beneficiary receives the assets only after the death of both owners. During the lifetime of the account owner(s), the beneficiaries have no interest in or control over the account and may not be given information regarding the account without authorization from the account owner(s). Registration of a security in beneficiary form may be cancelled or changed at any time by the owner or owners without the consent of the beneficiary. The TOD designation can name multiple beneficiaries, contingent beneficiaries and substitute beneficiaries, such as the grandchildren of a child who predeceases the owner. A trust is also a permissible beneficiary. Despite the utility of the new POD/TOD designations, they should not be used in place of sound estate planning. Stocks, bonds, and mutual funds should either be owned in trust or name the revocable living trust as beneficiary under a POD/TOD designation.

Uniform Transfer to
Minors Act (UTMA) Accounts

The Michigan Uniform Transfer to Minors Act ("UTMA")[46] permits a custodial account (bank account, mutual fund account, etc.) to be set up for the benefit of a minor. Any adult who is interested in the minor's financial future can establish an UTMA account and manage it as the account custodian. Account assets may be used for the minor's benefit as the custodian sees fit, including private school tuition or a new car. In general, account assets cannot be used to substitute for necessities for which parents are responsible, such as food, clothing and shelter.

Since the minor is considered the owner of the UTMA account, all of the unearned income generated by the asset is taxed at the minor's lower rate. For 2002, the first $750 of a minor's unearned income is income tax free. The next $750 is taxed at the minor's lower rate. Any unearned income above $1,500 is taxed at the parents' highest rate, if the minor is under age 14.

UTMA accounts have a number of drawbacks that, on balance, dictate against their use. It must be remembered that the custodian of an UTMA account must turn the assets of the account over to the minor no later than when the minor turns twenty-one (21). At that point, the minor can do with the assets as he or she pleases. Assets set aside for college may instead fund a sports car or a year on a tropical beach. An UTMA account may also adversely affect a child's ability to qualify for college financial aid. Finally, the UTMA account will be included in the estate of the gifting parent if the parent also acts as the custodian on the account.

Gifts made under the predecessor Uniform Gifts to Minors Act ("UGMA") – which was repealed and replaced in 1999 by UTMA – are now governed by the new UTMA rules, except that old UGMA gifts must be turned over to the minor at age *eighteen* (18) as required under UGMA. Despite the improvements made to UGMA by UTMA, such gifts have fallen out of favor. Now, Section 529 Plans are the preferred method of gifting to children.

Section 529 Plans

Section 529 plans – named after the section of the Internal Revenue Code from which they derive – are tax-favored educational savings plans. Contributions are not income tax deductible, but do qualify for the gift tax annual exclusion ($11,000 in 2002-2003). They can be pre-funded by con- tributing up to five years worth of gifts ($55,000) in one year. Earnings on contributions are not subject to income tax while in the plan, and are com- pletely forgiven if the withdrawals are used for qualified educational expenses. The original contributor can make withdrawals for his or her own use, but such withdrawals are not considered to be qualified and therefore are subject to income tax and penalties. Although established for a particu- lar beneficiary, the sponsor can change beneficiaries – if, for example the original beneficiary decides not to go to college – without tax or penalty. A plan set up by a grandparent does not count as part of the student's resources for financial aid purposes, and unlike an UTMA, plan assets are not part of the contributor's taxable estate.

Conclusion

Without proper planning, the forms of joint ownership or designation dis- cussed in this chapter can create unintended consequences at death. Assets passing by operation of law pass to the joint owner or named beneficiary immediately upon the death of the owner or joint tenant. Although such transfers avoid probate and delay, the opportunity to save tax, plan for minor (or handicapped) children, second spouses, and natural children is perma- nently lost. Assets passing by operation of law such as jointly owned assets, POD/TOD securities, assets that name a beneficiary, and UTMA accounts, are not controlled by the decedent's Will or revocable trust. Although mom's trust may direct that her entire estate be distributed to her three children equally, her assets may nonetheless pass to her daughter who lives nearby and whose name was added to mom's assets as a convenience to mom. The preferred approach to minimize estate tax, retain control of assets, insulate assets from children's creditors, and ensure that assets pass to the intended beneficiaries, it to re-title assets into a revocable living trust, rather than gamble on joint ownership and operation of law transfers.

Chapter 7

Why is probate so expensive and time consuming?

Probate courts have jurisdiction over the transfer of probate assets as they pass from the decedent to the decedent's heirs and beneficiaries. Probate courts also appointment guardians and conservators for minors and incompetents, and resolve disputes involving decedents estates. As with all courts in our judicial system, probate courts operate according to a complex set of procedures that, for the most part, require that the moving party be an attorney. Since Michigan probate attorneys typically charge between $150 and $250 per hour, the process gets expensive – fast.

Probate is a relatively expensive undertaking, primarily because it involves numerous filings with the probate court over an extended period of time. Probate is a creation of the Michigan legislature and is currently governed by a set of rules known as the "Estates and Protected Individuals Code" ("EPIC"). Probate laws are designed to administer estates in a manner that allows ample time for heirs, beneficiaries, creditors, and aggrieved parties to present their claims. For a relatively simple estate, the probate process takes approximately six months to one year (see example below). When disputes arise, as is often the case, probate can be substantially more expensive and protracted.

If the decedent died with a Will ("testate"), it must be filed with the probate court. If the court determines that the Will is genuine – it is in the proper form with the proper signatures – it will be "admitted" to probate and the court will officially appoint the personal representative. This initial process can be done either "formally" or "informally."

Informal probate may be used to appoint the personal representative if the person seeking appointment has legal priority over anyone else seeking appointment.[47] The person nominated by the decedent in the Will has first priority. If there is no Will, then a surviving spouse has priority. A document called an "Application for Probate" is filed (along with certain other documents) requesting appointment as personal representative. If the paperwork is in order, the court clerk will grant the Application and issue "letters of authority," which are used to show that the personal representative has the authority to handle the estate's business. A person without priority can also be appointed under the informal method if all interested parties consent.

Formal probate is required if the decedent died without a Will ("intestate") and no one with priority – like a surviving spouse – seeks appointment as personal representative. In the formal process, a petition is filed with the court. A hearing is then scheduled to rule on the petition and to appoint a personal representative. Notice of the hearing must be sent to all the interested parties at least 14 days prior to the hearing in order that all interested parties have ample opportunity to appear at the hearing to lodge their objection to the petition or appointment of personal representative. At the hearing the judge will listen to arguments for and against the appointment of the person as personal representative, and make a ruling.

Formal probate may be required where the decedent died with a Will if there are some deficiencies (e.g., missing signatures, alterations to the Will after execution) that prevent the informal admission of the Will, or may be elected if the petitioning party wants the judge to rule on the validity of the Will in order to eliminate any questions that could later arise.

Personal representatives have three basic duties: (1) to collect, preserve and value estate assets; (2) to pay debts, taxes, and administration expenses; and (3) to distribute the estate to the appropriate persons. The personal representative represents the estate in all matters including the preparation and filing of all income, gift, and estate tax returns.

A personal representative must use his or her best efforts and act in the best interest of the estate; protect and preserve the estate's assets; productively invest the assets of the estate; account for all income and expenses; keep interested parties informed of the progress of the estate's business; and ultimately distribute the estate to the beneficiaries named in the Will or to the heirs.

If appointed informally, the PR must give all of the decedent's heirs, beneficiaries and creditors notice of his or her appointment.[48] The interested parties may object to the PR's appointment and seek the appointment of another PR. Whether appointed formally or informally, the personal representative must regularly advise all interested parties of his or her actions. Naturally, all of the required notice and reporting requirements equate to more delay and attorney fees.

Probate proceedings – after admission of the Will and appointment of the personal representative – can be either *supervised or unsupervised.* In *supervised* probate, the court must approve all actions of the personal representative. Court approval requires appearances before the judge, and therefore more attorney involvement. Despite the added costs, personal representatives often choose supervised probate over unsupervised probate in order to insulate themselves from disgruntled heirs, beneficiaries or creditors. Since the court approves the personal representative's actions, parties who are unhappy with a particular action of the personal representative (e.g. sale of decedent's residence for a particular price or sale of an asset to one heir over another) will not be able to challenge the personal representative later.

In *unsupervised* proceedings, the personal representative handles the estate's business and it is up to the heirs or beneficiaries to bring any issues or problems to the court's attention. However, the personal representative can utilize all the procedures available in supervised administration to ask for court approval in advance of taking a particular action if the personal representative desires.

Where disputes are anticipated, "supervised" probate should be elected. "Unsupervised" probate is most appropriate where there is relative harmony in the family, and where no problem creditors are lurking.

Soon after appointment, the personal representative must publish notice of the decedent's death in a legal newspaper.[49] The newspaper notice is for the benefit of creditors of the estate and marks the beginning of the "publication period." A good part of the delay in probate results from the four-month publication period during which creditors of the decedent may make claims against the estate.[50] At the expiration of the publication period, creditors who have not filed claims are barred from asserting their claims.

The personal representative must make a reasonable attempt to locate creditors. Most creditors can be located from a simple review of the decedent's incoming mail or checkbook, or by contacting a credit agency to run a credit report. Known creditors must be sent a *Notice to Known Creditors.* Known creditors have one month from their receipt of the

Notice to Known Creditors (or four months from the date of the published *Notice to Creditors*, whichever is longer), to file a claim against the estate, or be forever barred. A known creditor who is not notified is not barred by the four-month time limit. Therefore, when in doubt, send a notice.

A personal representative may allow or disallow claims. Allowed claims are simply paid. Disallowed claimants must receive written notice of the disallowance. A disallowed creditor must file a lawsuit to further pursue its claim.

Probate provides a cutoff date for claims against the estate. Absent probate, creditors would be able to assert claims for up to three years after the death of the decedent (the statute of limitations on contract actions against an estate).[51]

Within 91 days of appointment, the personal representative must prepare a list of the estate's property called an "inventory." The inventory lists each item of property in the probate estate and its corresponding value. Personal items and household effects are often listed as a single entry with a single aggregate value. An "inventory fee," based on the aggregate value of the property listed on the inventory, is charged by the probate court. All beneficiaries and heirs are entitled to see the inventory.[52]

Each year the estate remains open, the personal representative must prepare, sign, and file federal and state income tax returns. Annual accountings of estate income and expense must also be prepared and filed with the court (supervised probate) or sent to beneficiaries and heirs (unsupervised probate). Most formal estates run their course in nine to eighteen months, requiring only one or two income tax filings.

Prior to final distribution in a supervised estate, a final accounting and an itemized list of proposed distributions must be prepared and sent to all interested parties and unpaid creditors. A hearing is held to approve the final accounting and proposed distributions. A party wishing to object to the personal representative's performance, or to the final distributions can do so at the hearing. Failure to object forever bars future complaints. Once approved by the court, final distributions can be made. It is advisable to obtain a receipt from each recipient showing that the distribution has been made.

Distributions in an unsupervised estate are handled much the same as in supervised probate, except that no hearing is required. A final account is sent to interested parties and creditors, along with receipts received at the time of distribution. Without a final hearing to cut off claims, creditors and disgruntled beneficiaries can bring an action years in the future. *For that reason, it is advisable to formally close an unsupervised probate estate.*

The duration and the cost of administering a probate estate will depend on a number of factors including the number of beneficiaries and the type, size and diversity of the estate's assets. Lack of cooperation from the parties or disputes among them can substantially prolong the estate administration process.

Ancillary probate in another state may be necessary if a Michigan decedent also owned real property in another state. In such cases, an ancillary probate proceeding in the state where the real estate is located would be necessary to obtain clear title to the real estate. For this reason, individuals with real estate in other states are strongly urged to transfer ownership of such real estate to a revocable living trust to avoid the necessity of probate in the state where the property is located.

Small Estates

Probate estates with total real and personal property valued at $17,000 or less may be eligible for a quick probate procedure (jointly held assets and assets that name a beneficiary are not counted toward the $17,000).[53] In Michigan, a *Petition and Order for Assignment* is filed. The law requires the assignment of the estate to the person who paid the funeral or burial expenses to the extent of the payment, with the balance going to the surviving spouse or, if there is no spouse, to the decedent's heirs.

The following time line identifies the more important dates in the administration of a "typical" *unsupervised* estate. Keep in mind that supervised probate takes even longer, because it involves court appearances, which must be scheduled and attended by interested parties.

Date of death	1/1/03
Letters of Authority are issued by the probate court appointing PR.	1/31/03
Notice of Appointment as PR and other documents must be sent to interested parties within **14 days** after appointment.	2/14/03
Date on which PR publishes notice to creditors of decedent's death and of time frame in which to file claims. Four (4) month publication period begins.	2/21/03

91 days after appointment of PR, PR must send copy
of estate inventory to interested parties.   5/1/03

4 months after notice to creditors is published,
creditors' claims are now barred and PR may proceed
to pay claims allowed against estate.   6/21/03

5 months after the PR is appointed is the earliest date
the estate may be closed.   6/30/03

6 months after the date of death is generally when the
decedent's assets may valued for federal estate tax
purposes (Alternate Valuation Date").   7/1/03

9 months after the date of death is the deadline to file
Federal and state estate tax returns and to pay
any tax due.   10/1/03

Date on which PR sends sworn statement
to interested parties.   11/15/03

Date on which PR has completed the transfer of
decedent's assets to interested parties.   11/15/03

Date on which PR filed sworn statement and proof
of service upon interested parties with court.   11/15/03

28 days after the sworn statement is filed is the deadline
for any interested parties to object to it; if no objection

is filed, the PR is entitled to receive a certificate that
he/she appears to have fully administered the estate.   12/13/03

Decedent's federal income tax return is due and
estate's federal income tax return is due.   4/15/03

Chapter 8

Do I need to retitle my assets after I create a revocable living trust?

The preparation of revocable trust documents is only the first step in eliminating probate and minimizing estate tax. Once drafted, trusts must be "funded" with the grantor's assets. The process of funding assets into trust can be somewhat laborious, but it is essential to achieving the full benefit of revocable trusts.

The method of transferring assets into trust will depend on the nature of the asset being transferred. For some assets, like stocks, bonds and real estate, the method of funding involves a change of *ownership*. Other assets, like qualified retirement plans and IRAs, do not permit a change of ownership during the lifetime of the grantor, and thus must be transferred into trust by means of a change of beneficiary. Whether by change of ownership or change of beneficiary, funding involves either a current or future change of ownership to the revocable living trust.

The name of the grantor, the trustee(s), and the date the trust are needed to identify the trust to which assets will be transferred. A typical trust name might be "Harry Barnes and Wendy Barnes (or Successor Trustee) as Trustees for the Harry Barnes revocable trust dated September 1, 2003, as amended." However, in light of the space limitations on ownership and beneficiary forms, it may be necessary to abbreviate the trust name down to its most important elements. The following name can be used in place of the full trust name described above: "Harry Barnes Trust dated 9/1/03."

For purposes of funding, assets can be broken into several broad categories:

Real Estate. Transferring ownership of real estate into trust is critical since real estate often comprises a significant portion of an individual's estate. A "warranty deed" is used to transfer real estate into trust. Grantor and the grantor's spouse, if married, transfer their entire interest in the real estate described in the deed to the "Grantee" named in the deed. For estate planning purposes, the grantee will either be the husband's revocable living trust or the wife's revocable living trust. In some cases, a one-half (1/2) interest will be transferred to each spouse's trust. The warranty deed below is a sample of real estate owned 1/2 by each spouse's trust. Note that current common practice is to use warranty deed – rather than a "quit claim deed" – to effectuate transfers of real estate to trust. Recent developments have raised concerns that the grantor's real estate title policy (insuring that grantor has clear legal title to his or her real estate) does not extend to the trust if a quit claim deed is used. A warranty deed solves this problem since a warranty deed guarantees clear title.

WARRANTY DEED

The Grantor(s)   Harry Barnes and Wendy Barnes, his wife

whose address is   14593 Burgess, Farmington, Michigan 48335

warranty(s) to an undivided one-half (1/2) interest in Harry Barnes, or his successor(s), as Trustee of the Harry Barnes Revocable Living Trust dated September 1, 2003, and an undivided one-half (1/2) interest in Wendy Barnes, or her successor(s), as Trustee of the Wendy Barnes Revocable Living Trust dated September 1, 2003.

whose address is   14593 Burgess, Farmington, Michigan 48335

the following described premises situated in the City of Farmington, Oakland County, Michigan:

        The North 60 feet Lot of, CASS LAKE GROVE SUBDIVISION, as recorded in Liber 15, Page 26 and 27, or Plats, Oakland County Records

for the sum of Exempt pusuant to MCLA 207.505(a) & MCLA 207.526(a)

Dated this 1st day of September, 2003

Signed in the presence of: Signed by:

_____   _____

P. MARK ACCETTURA   HARRY BARNES

_____   _____

KIMBERLY G. ANGERSTEIN   WENDY BARNES

The foregoing instrument was acknowledged before me this 1st day of September, 2003, by, Harry Barnes and Wendy Barnes, husband and wife

                          _____

                          P. MARK ACCETTURA
                          Notary Public, Oakland County
                          My commission expires 11/17/2006

When recorded Return to: Send Subsequent Tax Bills To: Drafted By:
P. MARK ACCETTURA   P. MARK ACCETTURA
35055 W. 12 Mile, #132   GRANTEE   35055 W. 12 Mile, #132
Farmington Hills, MI 48331   Farmington Hills, MI 48331

Tax Parcel #_____Recording fee_____   Transfer Tax _____

Once prepared, the warranty deed can either be "recorded" with the county, or simply held by the attorney or the client. Whether or not the warranty deed is recorded depends on a number of factors including the age of the grantor, how long the property is intended to be held, and the liability exposure of the grantor. Deeds of homeowners who intend to live in their home indefinitely should be recorded. Owners who intend to move or refinance may wish to leave their deed unrecorded since unrecorded deeds are not a matter of public record and thus do not complicate the sale or refinancing process. Unrecorded deeds can be recorded at a later date, even after the death of the grantor. As discussed in Chapter 19, *no* deed to trust should be prepared if the grantor believes that he or she will need long term nursing home care and intends to apply for Medicaid.

Married couples with significant liability exposure may choose to not record their warranty deed. Real estate owned by a husband and wife is "entireties" property (also know as a "tenancy by the entireties"), and is exempt from the individual creditors of either spouse. Titling real estate in one spouse's trust could expose the real estate to the claims of that spouse's creditors.

The fact that the real estate is subject to a mortgage is of no concern, since a later-filed deed does not affect the mortgage. Transfers to trust are exempt from state and local transfer taxes, and are not considered to be a taxable transfer for homestead tax assessment purposes. A principal residence owned in trust still qualifies for the $250,000/$500,000 forgiveness provisions of federal law. Note, however, that for Medicaid eligibility purposes, a principal residence owned by a revocable trust is *not* eligible for the homestead exemption (see Chapter 19).

Publicly Traded Securities. Ownership of publicly traded securities such as stocks, bonds and mutual funds whether held in the client's name or in a brokerage account should be transferred into trust. Stocks or bonds in "certificate" form (meaning that the investor holds the actual stock certificate or bond) should be re-registered in "street name." Securities held in street name are handed over to the financial institution, and a corresponding number of shares are credited to grantor 's trust account at the institution.

When making transfers of securities, the transfer agent, bank or brokerage house will ask for a copy of the trust. Clients are often reluctant to comply with this request feeling that such a request is both burdensome and an invasion of their privacy. Fortunately, a "Certification of Trust

Authority and Existence" may be presented to the financial institution in lieu of the actual trust document. A trust Certification is a summary of the essential terms of the revocable living trust document. A Certification conveys the essential information needed by the financial institution, while preserving the privacy of the grantor.

CERTIFICATION OF TRUST EXISTENCE AND AUTHORITY

STATE OF MICHIGAN)
OAKLAND COUNTY) ss

HARRY BARNES ("Grantor"), being first duly sworn, deposes and says as follows:

    1. That HARRY BARNES ("Grantor") created the HARRY BARNES revocable living trust under Agreement ("Agreement") dated September 1, 2003, which Agreement by its terms was subject to amendment or revocation by Grantor.

    2. The Grantor certifies that the Agreement remains in full force and effect.

    3. That the Trustees of the trust Agreement are set in the Agreement at Paragraph THIRTEENTH (a) as follows:

    (a) <u>Trustee Succession and Authority</u>. **HARRY BARNES** and **WENDY BARNES** are appointed as initial Trustees of this Trust Agreement. Either named - initial Trustee alone may conduct business on behalf of both Trustees, without the consent of the other initial Trustee. Upon the death or disability of either initial Trustee, the surviving or non-disabled Trustee shall act as sole Trustee. Upon the death or disability of both Trustee, **HARRY BARNES** and **WENDY BARNES**, Grantor's children, **DONNA BARNES** and **SAM BARNES** are herewith together designated as Successor Co-Trustee, with all of the rights, duties and powers herein created in and conferred upon the Trustee and/or Successor Trustee.

    4. That the Trustee and/or Successor Trustee(s), as the case may be, shall have all of the powers afforded Trustees under the Estates and Protected Individual Code (EPIC), 1998 PA 386.

    5. The legal description of the affected real property with regard to which this Certificate relates, if any, is attached hereto as Exhibit A.

WITNESSES:

_____

_____

             _____
             HARRY BARNES
             "GRANTOR/TRUSTEE"

_____

_____
             _____
             WENDY BARNES
             "TRUSTEE"

STATE OF MICHIGAN)
OAKLAND COUNTY) ss.

    On this 1st day of September, 2003, before me personally appeared HARRY BARNES and WENDY BARNES who, being first duly sworn, acknowledged that they executed the foregoing Certification of Trust Agreement as their own free act and deed and that they know the contents thereof.

             _____
             P. MARK ACCETTURA, Notary Public
             Oakland Country, Michigan
             My Commission Expires: 11/17/2006

Social Security Number. Revocable living trusts are treated as "grantor trusts," and are thus not subject to tax during the lifetime of the grantor. All income and loss from trust assets are reported on the grantor's personal income tax return (Form 1040 and MI 1040). Therefore, the grantor's social security number should be used as the tax identification number on all trust accounts.

Life Insurance. Life insurance should name the owner/insured's revocable living trust as beneficiary. This can be somewhat difficult to explain to married couples who instinctively believe that the surviving spouse is the proper beneficiary. Except in the case of transfers of life insurance to an irrevocable trust, it is not necessary to change the owner of the policy, simply changing the beneficiary will achieve the objective of funding the deceased owner/insured's revocable trust. A phone call from the owner of the policy to the insurance company requesting a "change of beneficiary form" will produce a change of beneficiary form in the mailbox of the owner/insured within three days of the call. For security reasons, insurance companies will not accept policy requests from anyone other than the owner. Finally, it is important to immediately return beneficiary designation forms since most companies will not honor beneficiary designation forms received after the death of the insured.

Non-publicly held Corporations, Partnerships, and LLCs. Closely held businesses, whether or not incorporated, often comprise a significant portion of the value of a decedent's estate. Potential buyers of the business after the death of the decedent need assurance that the successors in interest have the legal authority to sell the business asset. To avoid complications and delays after the death of the decedent, ownership of closely held businesses should be funded into trust during the lifetime of the owner. Canceling existing stock certificates and reissuing them in the name of the shareholder's revocable trust effectively transfers corporate ownership, as does amending the partnership agreement or the LLC operating agreement.

Qualified Retirement Plans, 401(k)s, SEPs, IRAs, 403(b)s. The owner (sometimes referred to as "participant") of a qualified retirement plan or other tax-preferred retirement savings accounts cannot be changed without causing the entire account to become immediately taxable to the owner. Artfully drafted beneficiary designation forms are necessary to properly fund retirement assets into trust while avoiding current income taxation. A careful reading of Chapter 17 is important to fully understand the interplay between the income and estate tax consequences of various beneficiary designations. As a rule of thumb, retirement assets require a two-part designation: The participant's spouse should be designated as the *primary* beneficiary, and the revocable trust of the participant should be named *contingent* beneficiary. A two-part beneficiary designation allows the greatest flexibility when negotiating the complex and perilous income and estate tax rules that apply to retirement plan assets (but see, Advanced Planning Caveat on page 99).

Personal Property. No action is required to fund personal property into trust. Being that personal property (e.g., furniture, jewelry, art work and other household items) cannot be re-titled (there's no deed for a table or chair!), such property cannot be transferred into trust. Instead, the decedent's Will governs the disposition of personal property. Most Wills permit the use of a "separate writing" disposing of items of personal property (See Chapter 4). Motor vehicles are specifically exempted from probate, and therefore do not need to be re-titled into the name of the revocable trust. Consequently, automobiles and other motor vehicles should not be transferred into trust. For liability purposes, the primary user of automobiles, recreation vehicles, and other motor vehicles should be named owner.

Often Missed Items. From the author's experience, there are three categories of often-missed assets: savings bonds, stock certificates, and undeveloped real estate lots. Savings bonds are often filed away and forgotten, as are stock certificates issued in the owner's name (said to be held in "certificate form"). Undeveloped lots are often a bad memory with little value, and therefore repressed from consciousness. Unfortunately, any one of these overlooked assets may require a probate proceeding to transfer title. For this reason, both the attorney and client must be diligent in identifying all assets of the estate.

Un-funded assets must pass through probate, and an un-funded trust is much less likely to preserve the grantor's Applicable Exclusion Amount. The attorney, client, and financial advisor need to work together in ensure full funding. Full participation of the client limits transfer costs and increases the likelihood that the trust(s) will continue to be properly funded long after the trust documents have been prepared.

The following chart summarizes the funding concepts discussed in this Chapter 8, using Harry and Wendy (husband and wife) as our sample estate planning couple.

TRUST FUNDING FOR HARRY AND WENDY

OWNERSHIP CHANGE   BENEFICIARY CHANGE

Description of asset	Current Ownership			Ownership Change		Beneficiary Change		Comments
	Harry	Wendy	Joint	Harry's Trust	Wendy's Trust	Primary Beneficiary	Secondary Beneficiary	
Harry's Employer 401(k)	X			Not Permitted	Not Permitted	Wendy	Harry's Trust	Law does not permit change of owner of IRA's and retirement Plans during lifetime. Naming spouse as primary beneficiary allows income tax rollover if spouse surviving. Participant's Trust as contingent beneficiary maximizes Trust funding.
Wendy's Employer 401(k)		X		Not Permitted	Not Permitted	Harry	Wendy's Trust	See above comment
Pension Plan Benefit-Lifetime Annuity w/ 60% Surviving Spouse Option	X			Not Permitted	Not Permitted	Wendy as Individual	N/A	Do nothing. Not an estate asset as long as pension by its terms ends at later of Harry and Wendy's death.
Life Insurance	X			NO	NO	Harry Trust	N/A	Fund in Trust of Owner/insured. May consider changing owner and beneficiary to Irrevocable Trust in larger estates.
IRA'S Harry	X				Not Permitted	Wendy	Harry Trust	Same rules as for 401(k). See above
Wendy		X		Not Permitted		Harry	Wendy Trust	
Real Estate Rental Property			X	X		N/A	N/A	Title in trust of Manager spouse. "Step-up" basis at death allows non-manager spouse to sell at death income tax free.
Residence			X	X	X	N/A	N/A	Use residence to equalize value of assets contained in H's and W's Trusts. Consider ½ ownership in each spouse's Trust as tenants in common.
Mutual Funds/Stocks			X	X	X	N/A	N/A	Title between H's and W's Trusts to equalize value of Trusts.
Checking Accounts			X	X	X	N/A	N/A	Leave in joint name unless there is a large balance. Consider adding Successor Trustee's name for easy access at death.
Savings Accounts			X	X	X	N/A	N/A	Title between H's and W's Trusts to equalize value of Trusts. Mutual funds and Stocks typically do not provide for the naming of a beneficiary.
Cars		X		NO	NO	N/A	N/A	Title cars in name of primary driver. Cars avoid probate. For liability reasons, do not transfer to Trust.
Safe deposit box			X	NO	NO	N/A	N/A	No longer "sealed" at death. Leave in joint name. Consider adding Successor Trustee's name.

Notes

Chapter 9

What is the maximum amount that I may gift per year without paying tax?

Gifts to friends, family members and charities are an effective way of reducing one's taxable estate. Some gifts are tax free, while others reduce the maker's ("donor's") "Applicable Exclusion Amount". Charitable gifts can also produce substantial income tax savings.

Annual Exclusion Gifts

Each individual may make annual gifts of up to eleven thousand ($11,000) dollars per calendar year per beneficiary without the imposition of federal gift tax.[54] The right to make annual tax-free gifts is known as the "annual exclusion." The annual gift tax exclusion is adjusted for inflation. However, it may be several years before the annual exclusion actually increases since the exclusion will rise only in increments of $1,000 and will be rounded to the next lowest multiple of $1,000 (i.e. if inflation pushes the amount to $11,999, it will be rounded down to $11,000).[55]

The tax code does not limit the number of beneficiaries to whom gifts can be made, nor does it require that the donee be related to the donor. Gifts may be made in cash or other property. Gift tax, if imposed, is the obligation of the donor. Gifts are almost always tax-free to the recipient.

If annual gifts to a single donor exceed $11,000, the gift tax annual exclusion covers the first $11,000 and only the excess is "taxable." However, rather than having to pay tax on the excess, taxable gifts reduce the donor's Applicable Exclusion Amount dollar for dollar. Each person has an Applicable Exclusion Amount sufficient to allow him or her to gift up to $1,000,000 (2002-2003) tax-free during life. Taxable gifts made during the donor's lifetime reduce the donor's Applicable Exclusion Amount available at death.

Taxable Gifts

The following example shows the effect of taxable gifts on the Applicable Exclusion Amount: Wendy gifts her son, Sam, $40,000 during 2002 from her separately owned assets. Assuming her spouse, Harry, did not consent to the gift, Wendy may only exclude $11,000 of the gift. The remaining $29,000 is "taxable." Accordingly, Wendy's Applicable Exclusion Amount is reduced by the amount of the taxable gift, to $971,000 ($1,000,000 - $29,000). Thus, Wendy's remaining Applicable Exclusion Amount allows her to leave $971,000, free of estate tax, at the time of her death.

Gift Splitting

A husband and wife may give $22,000 per beneficiary per year. This is true even where the gift is made entirely by one spouse, as long as the other spouse "consents" to the gift. A gift of jointly owned assets made by only one spouse is automatically deemed to have been made one-half by each spouse.[56] However, in cases where one spouse makes a $22,000 gift from separately owned assets, the spouses together must file IRS Form 709, in order to document the consent of the non-gifting spouse. In the above example, had Harry consented to Wendy's gift to Sam (by filing Form 709), both Harry and Wendy's Applicable Exclusion Amount would have been reduced by only $9,000, (40,000 - 22,000 = 18,000; 18,000 + 2 = 9,000) allowing them to each leave $991,000 estate tax free at death.

Exclusion for Educational and Medical Expenses

In addition to the $11,000 annual gift tax exclusion, there is an unlimited gift tax exclusion for direct payments of the donee's medical expenses or tuition.[57] The donor and donee need not be related to qualify either for the unlimited medical or educational exclusions. To qualify, payment must be made directly to the school, doctor or hospital that provides the service. A payment made to the donee will not qualify for the exclusion. A qualified educational organization is one that normally maintains a regular faculty and curriculum and normally has a regularly enrolled body of students (room and board, supplies, books and other fees do *not* qualify). Medical care includes expenses for diagnosis, cure, mitigation, treatment, or prevention of disease, as well as medical insurance.

The Marital Deduction

The unlimited marital deduction (see Chapter 10) allows spouses to make unlimited transfers to each other both during life and at death.[58] Unlimited transfers are not permitted, however, where the donee spouse is not a U.S. citizen or where gifts are of a "terminable interest." A terminal interest is an interest that, by its terms, will terminate and pass to someone other than the spouse. A classic example of a terminable interest is a gift of lifetime income to a spouse ("life estate"), with the "remainder" passing to children at the death of the spouse. An exception to the terminable interest rule applies to terminal gifts made to a trust that qualifies as a "QTIP" trust.[59] Gifts to a non-citizen spouse are limited to $100,000 annually.[60]

The "Present Interest" Requirement

To qualify for the annual $11,000 annual exclusion, a gift must be of a "present interest." A present interest is defined as the current right of a donee to the unrestricted enjoyment of the gifted asset. For example, Wendy's $11,000 outright gift to her son Sam, described above, would qualify for the gift tax exclusion. However, a transfer of $11,000 in trust for Sam to be distributed to Sam at the time of his mother's death, would not qualify as a gift of a present interest, since Sam would have no present right to the property. Sam would have only a future interest in the property, which vests on his mother's death.

The present interest rule poses special problems for transfers to irrevocable trusts. Irrevocable trusts typically own life insurance insuring the life of the grantor/settlor (the terms "grantor" and "settlor" are used interchangeably to designate the individual who created the trust). Life insurance premium payments are made to the trustee of the irrevocable trust, who in turn pays the annual premium to the life insurance company (see Chapter 15). Transfers to irrevocable trusts are certainly gifts, since the donor has made an irrevocable transfer, but they are not a gift of a present interest since the beneficiary of a typical irrevocable trust will not receive his or her share until the death of the settlor, when the life insurance death benefit is paid.

The present interest problem inherent in irrevocable trusts was solved in a court case involving a taxpayer named "Crummey." The *Crummey* case established the rule that if the beneficiaries of an irrevocable trust are given notice of contributions to the trust and are given an opportunity for a limited, but reasonable, period (typically 30 to 60 days), to withdraw their pro-rata share of the contribution, the transfer will be treated as a present interest. This "Crummey" power converts a taxable future interest gift to a gift of a present interest, and is one of the primary reasons for the popularity of irrevocable trusts to this day.

Trusts for Minors

A special exception to the normal present interest rule applies in the case of gifts in trust for the benefit of minor children. If: (1) the donee of the gift is a minor; (2) the terms of the trust provide that trust income and principal must be spent exclusively for the minor prior to the minor's attainment of age 21; (3) all remaining trust assets are to be paid to the minor at age 21; *and* (4) in the event of the death of the minor the trust assets are to be paid to the estate of the minor, then the annual exclusion is available despite the fact that the gift would otherwise be of a future interest.[61] The trust may also contain a clause permitting the donee to extend the term of the trust to beyond age 21.[62] This exception allows parents to qualify for the gift tax exclusion when they set assets aside in trust for future distribution to their children. From an income tax perspective, the income of such trusts is taxed at the parent's marginal tax rate if the trust beneficiary is less than fourteen years of age.

Charitable Gifts

Charitable gifts are income tax deductible. Charitable gifts also remove the gifted asset from the estate of the decedent. The nature of the gifted asset affects the amount of the income tax deduction, as does the type of charitable organization receiving the gift. See Chapter 18 for a complete discussion of charitable gift vehicles as well as the income tax deduction limits that apply to charitable gifts.

GRATS and GRUTS

GRATS and GRUTS present an opportunity to gift appreciating assets at a low gift tax cost. Basically, a GRAT (grantor retained annuity trust) and a GRUT (grantor retained unitrust) allow the donor to gift assets at a discount. Under both a GRAT and a GRUT, the donor retains an income interest for a period of years or for life, with the donee receiving the remaining trust assets ("remainder") at the end of the term. The gift is valued as of the date of the creation of the GRAT or GRUT. Since the gift is of the remainder, which is to be paid at a future date, the remainder is discounted. Using IRS tables,[63] the discount is determined by subtracting the value of the income interest from the value of the transferred asset. GRATS and GRUTS work best when funded with appreciating assets since the actual appreciation of the assets may far exceed the IRS discount rate (see example below).

Unfortunately the benefits of a GRAT or GRUT are lost if the donor fails to live to the end of the income term. Therefore, the duration of the trust must be carefully chosen to ensure that it is shorter than the life expectancy of the donor. However, the fact that the discount is directly tied to the retained income term (the longer the term the greater the discount) makes choosing a longer term tempting. The IRS has imposed rather strict rules relating to the calculation of the income interest retained by the grantor.[64] The rules of GRATS and GRUTS are amazingly similar to charitable split interest gifts discussed in Chapter 18.

Where the asset to be gifted is the donor's personal residence, the retained interest is the right of the donor to live in the home for a term of years or for the donor's life. Such arrangements are known as Personal Residence Trusts (PRTs) and Qualified Personal Residence Trusts (QPRTs).[65] Under a PRT or QPRT, the donor gifts his or her home to a named beneficiary (usually children) while retaining the right to live in the home. As with GRATs and GRUTs, the gift is valued as of the date the arrangement is created and discounted to account for the donor's retained interest. Tremendous tax savings can be achieved where the home is in a highly appreciating area.

> **Example:** Dad is a 65-year-old widower. He lives in a $300,000 home that has been appreciating an average of 6% per year. Dad would like to live in the home ten (10) more years and then move to senior housing. Dad creates a QPRT, gifting his home to his children while retaining the right to live in the home for ten (10) years. Based on IRS tables, the value of the gift to the children is $128,154. The value of the home when received by the children in ten (10) years will actually be $537,254 (based on 6% annual growth). Note that the tax benefits of the entire arrangement are wiped out if Dad fails to live 10 years.

Planning Strategy

Prior to passage of EGTRRA in 2001, an important estate tax savings strategy of individuals with larger estates was to make *taxable gifts* of appreciating assets. The thinking was that the earlier highly appreciating assets were removed from the taxpayer's estate – even if gift tax was incurred – the greater the estate tax savings. Making taxable gifts to the extent of one's Applicable Exclusion Amount continues to be sound estate tax planning. However, it is hard to justify paying tax on gifts that exceed the Applicable Exclusion Amount with the repeal of the estate tax in 2010 lurking. Interestingly, even as the Applicable Exclusion Amount for transfers at death is scheduled to rise to $3.5 million in 2009, with possible estate tax repeal in 2010, the *gift tax* exemption (which is in addition to the annual $11,000 exclusion on present interest gifts) is *never* scheduled to rise above $1,000,000. See Chapter 12 for a complete discussion of the Applicable Exclusion Amount and the taxable limits on gifts.

There are important *income* tax considerations when making gifts. A gift given during life "carries over" the tax basis of the donor. For example, if Wendy gifts XYZ Corporation stock to her son, for which she paid $10 per share, and her son sells the stock for $50, he will have a reportable capital gain of $40. Wendy's basis of $10 is said to "carry over" to her son, which he uses to calculate his gain on the sale of the stock. If instead, Wendy left XYZ stock to her son at death, he would receive a "stepped-up" basis (see Chapter 11 for a complete discussion of "basis"). Obviously, Wendy's son is further ahead – *from an income tax standpoint* – if he receives the XYZ stock at his mother's death rather than as a gift. Beginning in 2010, only $1,300,000 of a decedent's assets will receive a stepped up basis ($4,300,000 for surviving spouses).

Lifetime giving requires an analysis of both the income and estate tax consequences of each gift. The analysis has never been more difficult when one considers the uncertain future of the gift and estate tax laws. Donors employing the taxable gift strategy should consider utilization of a limited liability company to allow the donor to continue to control the gifted assets and to take advantage of the valuation discounts available for such transfers (see Chapter16).

Chapter 10

What is the most I can give to my spouse tax-free during my lifetime or at death?

Transfers between spouses are gift and estate tax free by virtue of the "unlimited marital deduction."[66] Spouses may make unlimited lifetime gifts to each other, and may leave the other an unlimited amount at death tax free. The unlimited marital deduction is the reason that there is rarely any estate tax on the death of the first spouse to die.

To qualify for the marital deduction, a gift or bequest may not be "terminable."[67] That is, the transfer may not be subject to some future contingency such as the subsequent death or remarriage of the surviving spouse. For example, a transfer in trust for the surviving spouse "unless she remarries" does not qualify for the marital deduction.

Transfers that qualify for the marital deduction basically fall within three categories: (1) outright transfers to the surviving spouse; (2) transfers in trust for the benefit of the surviving spouse over which he or she has a "general power of appointment"; and (3) transfers into a Qualified Terminable Interest Property ("QTIP") trust. Outright transfers are self-explanatory; the other transfers that qualify for the unlimited marital deduction are discussed below.

Power of Appointment Trusts

A transfer in trust over which the surviving spouse has a general power of appointment can best be explained by example:

Husband has an estate of $1,150,000. He leaves $1,000,000 outright to his children and places the balance ($150,000) in a marital trust. The marital trust provides that all income and principal are to be used for the benefit of the surviving spouse during her lifetime with the balance remaining in trust at her death to pass to the beneficiaries *she* designates in her Will.

The marital trust in the above example contains a general power of appointment since the surviving wife has the power to appoint beneficiaries of her choosing at the time of her death. The $150,000 principal of the marital trust qualifies for the marital deduction, thereby passing estate tax-free to the surviving spouse.

QTIP Trusts

The QTIP marital deduction is a relatively recent creation (1981), and was designed to address the needs of the changing American family. The traditional forms of marital deduction described above (outright transfer and general power of appointment) were not thought to be appropriate in second marriage situations. It was believed that if the surviving spouse was required to have a general power of appointment or received an outright distribution of the marital portion, the surviving spouse would not name the first spouse's children as beneficiaries of the balance of the marital trust at his or her death.

To be qualified, all income of the QTIP must be distributed to the surviving spouse at least annually, and the principal of the trust may not be used for any beneficiary other that the surviving spouse during the surviving spouse's lifetime.[68] Upon the death of the surviving spouse, the QTIP distributes to the beneficiaries named by the first spouse.

QTIPs strike a balance between the financial needs of the surviving spouse and the deceased spouse's wish to leave an inheritance to his or her children. QTIPS are especially beneficial in second marriage situations where the interests of the surviving spouse and the children of the decedent may be adverse. A QTIP trust does not permit the surviving spouse to appoint QTIP assets at death.

Non-citizen Spouses

Special estate planning is required for non-U.S. citizens.[69] No marital deduction is available if the surviving spouse is not a U.S. citizen, and only a limited marital deduction is permitted for lifetime gifts to a non-citizen spouse. Thus, special planning is necessary where one or both spouses is not a citizen of the United States. Often the best advice for couples that intend to permanently reside in the U.S. is to apply for and receive

U.S. citizenship. Alternatively, a Qualified Domestic Trust ("QDOT") may be used to qualify for the marital deduction in situations where the non-citizen spouse does not wish to obtain U.S. citizenship. Property passing to a non-citizen spouse *is* eligible for the Applicable Exclusion Amount ($1,000,000 in 2002-2003).

Estate tax on assets qualifying for the marital deduction is not forgiven; it is merely postponed. Assets qualifying for the marital deduction are included in the estate of the surviving spouse. Outright distributions are also included in the surviving spouse's estate since the surviving spouse is the outright owner of the asset. Assets over which the surviving spouse has a power of appointment are included by virtue of the rule that includes in the estate of the decedent all assets over which the decedent has a general power of appointment.[70] QTIP assets are included in the estate of surviving spouse by virtue of a special Internal Revenue Code ("Code") provision requiring such inclusion.[71]

Congress recognized that it would be unfair to include QTIP assets in the estate of surviving spouse, yet distribute such assets to the predeceased spouse's children. To solve this inequity, the Code allows the estate of the surviving spouse to recover the additional estate tax resulting from the inclusion of the QTIP assets in the surviving spouse's estate from the QTIP beneficiaries.[72]

For all of its apparent advantages, reliance on the unlimited marital deduction can actually result in higher overall estate tax. Without proper planning, the first spouse to die may simply leave everything to his or her surviving spouse. Although there would be no estate tax on the death of the first spouse, the couple may have set themselves up for a much higher tax on the surviving spouse's death. By passing the entire estate to the surviving spouse, the couple would fail to take advantage of the $1,000,000 Applicable Exclusion Amount (2002-2003) of the deceased spouse. In larger estates (over $1,000,000), it is important that each spouse adopt a revocable living trust to fully utilize *each* spouse's Applicable Exclusion Amount (See Chapter12).

Notes

Chapter 11

Do you have to pay income tax on inherited assets? What is a "stepped-up basis"?

Beneficiaries and heirs are often surprised to learn that, for the most part, inherited assets are received income tax free.[72.1] The primary exception to this general rule is income in respect of a decedent ("IRD"). IRD includes pension, IRA and 401(k) distributions, certain annuity payments and the decedent's final paycheck.[73] Other than IRD, most other assets received from a decedent, including the proceeds of life insurance,[74] are received income tax free.

Stepped-up Basis
The Law Until 2010

In addition to being income tax free, the appreciation on capital assets received from a decedent is also forgiven.[75] The tax mechanism that allows for the forgiveness of appreciation is the "step-up" in basis.[76] A step-up in basis allows the beneficiary to sell an asset received from a decedent income tax free. In order to understand basis step-up, one must first understand the concept of "basis."

Basis is an individual's investment in an asset. The starting point in calculating one's basis is to determine the asset's original cost.[77] For example, if Harry paid $10,000 for a stock, and sold it for $20,000, his gain would be $10,000. Harry's amount realized ($20,000) less his basis ($10,000) equals his gain. Basis is the mechanism used to measure gain or loss on the sale of an asset.

An individual's basis in an asset can change over time. An addition to a residence, for example, would increase the owner's basis in the residence. By contrast, the basis of rental real estate is reduced by the amount of depreciation taken by the taxpayer.[78]

If an appreciated asset were sold prior to death, the owner would be liable for income tax on the appreciation. By contrast, an inherited asset receives a stepped-up (or step-down) basis (see Chapter 18 for strategy of selling highly appreciated assets tax free after transfer to a Charitable Trust). That is, the beneficiary is deemed to have paid the fair market date-of-death value for the inherited asset. If the beneficiary sells the inherited asset immediately, he or she would have no income tax liability with respect to such sale. A stepped-up basis eliminates any income tax consequences associated with the sale of inherited property by the beneficiary.

The combination of the stepped-up basis rules, and the tax-free nature of inheritances, generally results in no income tax being due on inherited assets (other than income in respect of a decedent). If the beneficiary sells the inherited asset at some future date, his or her gain, if any, is only the appreciation since decedent's date of death.

The step-up basis rules were created to avoid double tax. The thinking was that assets included in the decedent's estate should not also be subject to income tax. Interestingly, the stepped-up basis rules apply even if no estate tax is owed.

A full step-up in basis occurs when an asset is held solely in the name of the decedent.[79] Different rules apply where an asset is held jointly. If the joint tenant is the decedent's spouse, the surviving spouse receives a stepped-up basis equal to one-half of the date-of-death value of the asset[80] no matter which spouse supplied the original consideration needed to acquire the asset.

Assets held jointly between the decedent and a non-spouse receive a step-up in basis to the extent that the decedent supplied the original consideration for the asset.[81] For example: Mom adds her son, Sam, as a joint tenant on her home for which she supplied the entire purchase price. On Mom's death, the entire value of the home would be included in Mom's estate due to the fact that she retained the right to live in the home (see Chapter 2),[82] and Sam would receive a stepped-up basis equal to the entire value of the home. If Sam were to predecease his mother, Sam's mother would not receive any step-up in basis. The residence would not be included in Sam's estate (since he supplied no part of the purchase price), and therefore Mom's interest acquired from Sam does not receive a stepped-up basis.

Carry-over Basis
The Law Beginning in 2010

Under EGGTRA, up to $1,300,000 of decedent's estate receives a step-up (plus an additional $3,000,000 for property left to a surviving spouse). The decedent's personal representative or trustee may elect – in a filing with the IRS – the assets to which the step-up applies. Assets in excess of $1,300,000 (or $4,300,000 for married couples) carry decedent's basis – a "carry-over" basis. For example (ignoring for the moment the step-up on $1,300,000 or $4,300,000): if Douglas bought XYZ Company stock for $20 per share in 1965, and dies in 2010 when the stock is worth $72 per share, his heirs will have a basis of $20 per share. If they later sell the stock for $80 per share, they will have to pay income tax on a gain of $60 per share. If the stock received a stepped up basis at Douglas' death, the gain would only be $8 per share.

As presently structured, the carry-over basis rules will only be in effect for the year 2010 since – absent congressional intervention – the provisions of EGGTRA sunset in 2011 (see Chapter 12).

Alternate Valuation Date

Rather than valuing the decedent's property on the date of the decedent's death, the decedent's personal representative may elect to use the "Alternate Valuation Date." The Alternate Valuation Date ("AVD") is the date that is six months after the date of the decedent's death.[83] The AVD is extremely useful in situations where, shortly after death, the decedent's assets significantly decline in value. The impact of electing the alternate valuation date is twofold: 1) the value of the estate's assets are reduced for estate tax purposes; and 2) the basis of assets received by the beneficiary are determined as of the AVD. If the AVD is elected, *all* assets of the decedent must be valued as of the AVD. The personal representative cannot pick and choose which assets will be valued at death and which will be valued as of the AVD. However, any property disposed of during the six month period between date of death and the alternate valuation date will be valued (and its basis determined) as of the date of disposition.

Deathbed Transactions

Basis stepped-up is denied if the property was acquired by the decedent by gift within one year of his or her death, and the property passes back to the donor at the decedent's death.[84] In such cases, the donor/beneficiary retains his or her original basis and cannot utilize the stepped-up basis rule. The exception prevents manipulation of the step-up basis rules for the benefit of the surviving taxpayer. Such would be the case if taxpayers were allowed to make gifts to dying people with the understanding that they would receive the gifted asset back at death with a new fair market value basis.

> **Example:** Son, Sam, owns property with a basis of $1,000 and a fair market value of $20,000. Sam gifts the property to Mom who is terminally ill, Mom takes Sam's $1,000 basis. Mom dies less than one year later and leaves the property to Sam in her Will. Under the deathbed exception to the step-up rules, Sam's basis is $1,000, not $20,000.

Income in Respect of a Decedent

Income in respect of a decedent ("IRD") is income earned by a decedent, but not paid to the decedent before death.[85] Examples of IRD include: interest on U.S. savings bonds, deferred compensation, decedent's final pay check, bonuses, stock options, and retirement plan distributions.[86] As noted above, beneficiaries receiving IRD must pay regular income tax at their personal income tax rate in the year of receipt. The stepped-up basis rules do not apply to IRD. To prevent double taxation, the recipient of IRD is allowed an income tax deduction equal to the portion of the estate tax paid by the decedent's estate attributable to the IRD item.[87]

IRD makes an ideal bequest to charity. Charities, being tax exempt, keep every dollar of such tax-burdened assets. Since IRD assets may be subject to tax at the rate of over 70% (estate tax plus income tax), they should be the first option when choosing assets to bequest to charity. It is important that IRD items be specifically referenced in the decedent's Will or trust as passing to the charity, or that the charity be directly named as beneficiary of the IRD item. Otherwise, satisfying a pecuniary bequest to a charity (e.g., "I leave $100,000 to the Salvation Army") out of IRD items will generate an estate tax charitable deduction but the estate will have to include the IRD in *its* income.[88]

Chapter 12

What is the most I can leave estate tax free to my children?

The answer to this question has become a lot more complex since passage of the Economic Growth and Tax Relief Reconciliation Act (EGTRRA) of 2001. Basically, the amount a decedent can leave estate tax free depends on the Applicable Exemption Amount that corresponds to the year of decedent's death. Assuming EGTRRA continues in its present form, the analysis breaks down to three time periods: 2002-2009; 2010; and post 2011.

2002-2009

For the period 2002-2009, the amount that can be passed estate tax free starts at $1,000,000 in the year 2002 and grows to $3,500,000 by the year 2009, as illustrated on the following chart:

Year of Transfer	Applicable Exemption Amount	Gift Tax Exemption
2002	$1,000,000	$1,000,000
2003	$1,000,000	$1,000,000
2004	$1,500,000	$1,000,000
2005	$1,500,000	$1,000,000
2006	$2,000,000	$1,000,000
2007	$2,000,000	$1,000,000
2008	$2,000,000	$1,000,000
2009	$3,500,000	$1,000,000
2010	Estate Tax Repealed	$1,000,000
2011	$1,000,000	$1,000,000

An unlimited amount – over and above the Applicable Exemption Amount – can be passed to a surviving spouse[89] (the "unlimited marital deduction"). Without proper planning, these two seemingly generous rules can offset each other. For example, if a decedent leaves all of his assets to his surviving spouse (as would be the case where spouses hold all of their assets jointly), the decedent permanently forfeits his right to leave $1,000,000 (2002) estate tax free to individuals other than his or her surviving spouse.

If a couple's combined estates exceed the Applicable Exemption Amount, it is important that they plan together to fully utilize their respective Applicable Exemption Amounts. With proper planning, they may leave up to double the Applicable Exemption Amount ($2,000,000 in 2002) free of federal estate tax. To accomplish this result, and gain the full benefit of both spouses' Applicable Exemption Amount, each spouse must have a revocable living trust.

Once created, each trust must be "funded" (see Chapter 8). That is, the couple's assets must be re-titled into the name of their trusts – with an eye toward making them roughly equal in value. The diagram below illustrates the operation of the two-trust system. Each trust is funded with assets previously owned by the couple either individually or in joint name. During the lifetime of the spouses, the family and marital trusts are dormant and do not become operational until the death of the grantor.

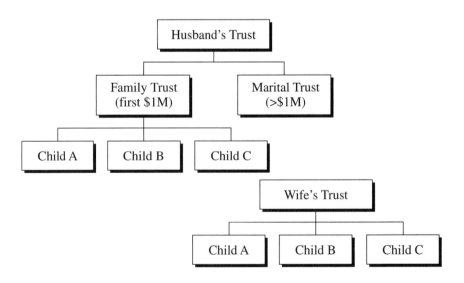

Upon the death of the first spouse to die (the "husband" in the above example), the deceased spouse's trust divides into two separate trusts: the "family trust" and the "marital trust." According to the terms of the typical revocable living trust, trust assets equal to the Applicable Exemption Amount ($1,000,000 in 2002) are first allocated to the family trust, with the balance (if any) allocated to the marital trust. No federal estate tax is due on the death of the husband, since the husband's Applicable Exemption Amount covers the family trust, and the marital trust qualifies for the unlimited marital deduction. *No marital deduction is available if the surviving spouse is a non-U.S. citizen.*[90] It should be noted that the balance remaining in the marital trust upon the wife's subsequent death is included in the wife's estate for tax purposes. The marital trust, may, by its terms, permit the surviving spouse to designate the beneficiary of the balance of the marital trust at the surviving spouse's death (a "general power of appointment") or may not permit such designation ("QTIP" Trust, See Chapter 10).

The surviving spouse may never designate the beneficiary of the balance of the family trust, since such power would cause the family trust to be included in the estate of the surviving spouse. Such a result would defeat the purpose of creating the family trust; that is, to bypass the surviving spouse and utilize the Applicable Exemption Amount of the first spouse to die.

After the first spouse's death, income and principal from both the family trust and the marital trust are available to the surviving spouse to allow her to maintain the lifestyle she enjoyed while her husband was alive. Typically, amounts remaining in the marital trust *at the time of the surviving spouse's death* are paid over to the husband's family trust to be added to other family trust assets and thereafter allocated among the beneficiaries of the family trust. As noted above, amounts transferred to the marital trust qualify for the marital deduction as long as the surviving spouse has either a general power of appointment or the marital trust qualifies as a QTIP. In the event that the marital trust is drafted to contain a general power of appointment in the surviving spouse, the surviving spouse could in fact appoint her own beneficiaries to receive the amounts remaining in the marital trust at the time of her death. Power of appointment marital trusts provide that in the absence of a specific exercise of the power of appointment in the surviving spouse's Will, amounts remaining in the marital trust at the death of the surviving spouse will automatically be transferred to the family trust to be distributed according to the terms of the family trust.

The two-trust system described above allows couples to shelter of up to $2 million (2002) from federal estate tax. Various planning techniques are available to estates that exceed $2 million. Irrevocable life insurance trusts act to remove the full value of life insurance from the decedent's estate (see Chapter 15). Limited liability companies are proven vehicles for making lifetime gifts while allowing the donor to retain control over the gifted assets (see Chapter16). Charitable Trusts allow for substantial income and estate tax savings for the charitable minded (see Chapter18).

Couples with a combined estate that is substantially below $1,000,000 should consider adopting a "joint" revocable living trust. Such trusts avoid probate and deliver all of the other non-tax benefits of revocable living trusts. Joint trusts become irrevocable only on the death of the *surviving spouse* and thus eliminate much of the administrative burdens of irrevocable trusts (see Chapter Seven: *Lost and Found: Finding Self-Reliance After the Death of a Spouse*, Collinwood Press, 2001).

Michigan converted to a "pick up" estate tax in 1993,[91] effectively eliminating Michigan Inheritance tax. Now, the State of Michigan receives a portion of the federal estate tax that would have been paid the federal government if not for the state death tax credit available on the federal return (Form 706).[92] EGTRRA phases out the state death tax credit by the year 2005. States like Michigan that adopted a pick up tax will either have to forego all inheritance revenues after 2004 or reinstate their old inheritance tax regimes. Thus, EGTRRA not only creates uncertainty at the federal level, but the state level as well.

The federal estate tax, when it applies, is rather severe. As with the federal income tax, the federal estate tax is graduated, with larger estates subject to a higher percentage of tax.[93] As can be seen below, the federal estate tax can reach fifty (50%) percent. The first step in calculating the federal estate tax is to calculate the tentative tax. The decedent's unified credit from the Applicable Exemption Amount is then applied to offset the tax. The tentative tax is determined by applying the tax rates from the table on the next page to the decedent's taxable estate (see Chapter 2 for the method of determining taxable estate).

The unified rate schedule, with adjustments noted at the bottom of the schedule that reflect the phased-in reduction of the maximum transfer tax rates, applies to estates of decedents dying, and gifts made, after 1983, but before January 1, 2010. EGTRRA repealed the estate tax with respect to estates of decedents dying *after* December 31, 2009.

ESTATE AND GIFT TAX TABLE

If the amount is:

Over (1)	But not over(2)	Tax on (1)	Rate on Excess (1)
$ 0	$ 10,000	$ 0	18
10,000	20,000	1,800	20
20,000	40,000	3,800	22
40,000	60,000	8,200	24
60,000	80,000	13,000	26
80,000	100,000	18,200	28
100,000	150,000	23,800	30
150,000	250,000	38,800	32
250,000	500,000	70,800	34
500,000	750,000	155,800	37
750,000	1,000,000	248,300	39
1,000,000	1,250,000	345,800	41
1,250,000	1,500,000	448,300	43
1,500,000	2,000,000	555,800	45
2,000,000	2,500,000	780,800	49
2,500,000	3,000,000	1,025,800	53
3,000,000	3,500,000	1,290,800	55

The two highest tax brackets of 53 percent and 55 percent apply to estates of decedents dying, and gifts made, on or before December 31, 2001. For estates of decedents dying, and gifts made, after December 31, 2001, the maximum tax rate is 50%.

Calculating the Tax

For example, if Harry died in 2002 with an estate of $1,300,000, his tentative tax would be $469,800 ($448,300 plus 43% of the excess over $1,250,000). If Harry had not used any of his unified credit during his lifetime, his full $345,800 unified credit would be applied against his tentative tax ($469,800 - $345,800) leaving an actual federal estate tax of $124,000.

Had Harry died in 2002 with an estate of $1,000,000, his tentative tax would have been $345,800, exactly equal to the unified credit for 2002. The credit would exactly offset the tax due. For sake of simplicity, speakers and writers on the subject of estate planning often refer only to the Applicable Exclusion Amount ($1,000,000) and not the actual unified credit amount ($345,800).

2010

EGTRRA fully repeals the estate tax in the year 2010. If death occurs in 2010, no tax is due no matter what the size of the decedent's estate. Note, however, that the gift tax is *not* repealed. Apparently, Congress retained the gift tax to discourage the gifting of income-producing assets to family members in lower income tax brackets for income tax avoidance purposes.

2011 and Forward

EGTRRA contains a sunset provision: changes contained in the act *expire* on December 31, 2010 unless Congress and the President ratify the Act before that date. If the sunset takes effect, all of EGTRRA's changes would be repealed; the law would revert to its pre-2001 status, and the Applicable Exemption Amount would return to $1,000,000. Planning is difficult with the looming sunset provision. One cannot assume that the estate tax will disappear in 2010, especially considering how the world has changed since EGTRRA's passage. Remember that the major impetus for the elimination of the estate tax in 2001 was the budget surplus that was predicted to last far into the future. Today, the budget surplus, thriving economy and stock market have vanished, while domestic and military defense costs have skyrocketed. With a widening budget deficit, it is only be a matter of time before Congress revisits the tax code looking for revenue. Democrats and Republicans will undoubtedly propose different solutions, but changes in some form are inevitable. From an estate planning perspective, the only prudent approach in to assume that the estate tax will be with us for a very long time to come, and individuals with estates in excess of $1,000,000 should continue to plan to minimize or eliminate estate tax.

Qualified Family Owned Business Interest Exclusion

The 1997 Tax Act created the "Qualified Family Owned Business Interest Exclusion," ("QFOBI Exclusion").[94] The exclusion increases the total individual exclusion amount to $1.3 million and could potentially increase a married couple's total exclusion amount to $2.6 million, if an estate contains certain family owned business assets. The QFOBI exclusion – due to its unnecessary complexity – never delivered the tax relief hoped for, and under EGTRRA is repealed effective January 1, 2004.

Chapter 13

Are there special estate planning considerations where there has been a second marriage?

Second marriages present special challenges in estate planning, especially when children from prior marriages are involved. Estate planning for such couples is a balancing act between the needs of the surviving spouse and to one's natural children. The surviving spouse must be assured that he or she will be able to maintain the lifestyle the couple enjoyed while both spouses were alive. At the same time, biological children must be properly remembered.

Multiple marriage spouses cannot afford to take the "do nothing" approach, or the joint ownership approach (see Chapter 6) to estate planning. The messiest probate battles almost always involve stepparents, stepchildren, and stepsiblings. Parents who have the attitude: "I don't care what happens after I'm gone…I'm dead," leave a legacy of hurt feelings and anger. Families are often permanently divided into warring camps. Worse yet, expensive and emotionally draining probate litigation can sometimes diesel on for years. If you love your family, don't leave *them* to sort out your estate mess. With proper planning, the estates of multiple marriage spouses can be administered in an orderly, mature fashion, with provision made for all interested parties.

The needs and wishes of couples in second marriages vary widely, depending on the age of the spouses, their net worth, the length of their marriage, the age of their children, and their relative contributions to the marital estate. In most cases, separate revocable living trusts (one for each spouse) with QTIP provisions will accomplish the varied needs of the couple. Prenuptial and postnuptial agreements are recommended where the spouses make little or no provision for each other at death.

Ethical Considerations

Sometimes, the interests of the couple are so diverse that one attorney cannot represent both spouses. Ethically, an attorney acting on behalf of both spouses cannot keep confidential information disclosed by one spouse from the other spouse.[95] The attorney must either withdraw representation from both spouses, or, with prior approval, disclose the information to the other spouse. It is the attorney's responsibility to recognize conflicts of interest. Spouses should nevertheless discuss ethical issues with the attorney up front in order to avoid any inadvertent partiality on the part of the attorney.

Prenuptial and Postnuptial Agreements

Prenuptial (sometimes also called "Antenuptial") and postnuptial agreements are essential estate planning tools. Prenuptial or postnuptial agreements (prenuptial before marriage and postnuptial after marriage) override state law with respect to the division of marital assets on death or divorce (see Michigan Statutory Rights below). By law, one attorney cannot represent both spouses in the preparation of a prenuptial or postnuptial agreement.[96]

Prenuptial agreements have long been enforceable with regard to the division of assets upon the death of a spouse.[97] Now, Michigan – and the other 49 states – recognizes the validity of premarital agreements in divorce.[98]

Spouses may agree to leave all of their assets to their children at death, and little, if any, to each other. This might be the case where a couple, married later in life, has each brought substantial assets to the marriage. Without a prenuptial or postnuptial agreement, the wishes of such a couple may not be achieved. Michigan law would allow the surviving spouse to take his or her "marital share" of the deceased spouse's estate, at the expense of the deceased spouse's children.

A surviving spouse may assert his or her statutory rights even where the spouses had informally agreed otherwise during life. Estate planning documents that fail to address statutory rights can also be challenged. Only properly drafted trust documents and valid prenuptial or postnuptial agreements can prevent the surviving spouse from taking up to one-half of the amount intended to pass to the children of the deceased spouse.

Several conditions must be met for a Prenuptial or Postnuptial agreement to be valid under Michigan law:[99] (1) The agreement must be in writing; (2) each party must make full disclosure of his and her personal financial information, including assets and income; (3) each party must be represented by separate independent legal counsel; (4) the agreement must be voluntarily entered into without fraud, mistake or duress (to prevent the appearance of duress, the prenuptial agreement should not be executed on the eve of the marriage); and (5) the agreement must be fair when entered into.

Prenuptial and postnuptial agreements allow spouses to agree on a number of important issues including: (1) how to segregate assets brought into marriage; (2) how assets acquired during the marriage will be owned; (3) who will be responsible for debt acquired during the marriage; (4) how living expenses will be shared; (5) how assets will be distributed at the death or divorce of the spouses; and (6) who will be responsible for income tax.

Separate Trusts

Revocable living trusts are a valuable tool in preserving the wishes of the grantor. Only the grantor of a revocable living trust may amend the trust agreement. Upon the death or disability of the grantor, the trust becomes irrevocable, since the only person who had the right to amend the trust – the grantor – has passed. To the extent that each spouse has separate and distinct wishes, they should each have a separate revocable trust that locks in their wishes upon their death or permanent disability.

Even without a prenuptial or postnuptial agreement, spouses can protect their separate interests in assets brought into the marriage. Separate assets funded in each spouse's separate revocable living trust, and subsequently maintained in that trust during the course of the marriage, remain separate in divorce.[100] Michigan law does not consider assets funded in a revocable trust to be part of the decedent's estate for purposes of calculating the surviving spouse's elective share.[101] Thus, a funded trust will frustrate, if not defeat, a surviving spouse's right to a statutory share.

Choice of Trustee

Trustees have a fiduciary obligation to strictly implement the terms of the trusts over which they have been appointed. Deliberate misuse or mismanagement of trust assets can result in civil, and even criminal, penalties. Revocable trusts prepared by the author typically appoint spouses as initial co-trustee, granting each spouse equal and independent power while both are alive and able. Upon the death or disability of one spouse, the surviving or non-disabled spouse acts as sole trustee.

The surviving spouse may, however, not be a suitable successor trustee in second marriage situations. For instance, if the relationship between the children of the deceased spouse and the surviving spouse breaks down, who will monitor the actions of the surviving spouse/trustee? The children may not learn of the surviving spouse's misuse of trust assets until after the surviving spouse's death, when it's too late. Although certain statutory reporting requirements would require the surviving spouse to account to the children annually, enforcement of these rights would require the children to take their step parent to court.

To avoid conflict, a neutral third party, like a bank or brokerage house, should be considered as successor trustee. The surviving spouse could also be appointed as co-trustee with a family member of the deceased spouse. Only the spouses themselves can answer the question of who is an appropriate successor trustee. They will have to agree on a suitable solution based on their level of trust, and their relationship with their respective step children.

QTIP Trusts

QTIP trusts were created specifically to address second marriage situations (see Chapter 10). A QTIP trust allows the surviving spouse to enjoy the income from the marital trust during his or her lifetime, with no power to appoint the balance remaining in the marital trust at his or her death. Using a QTIP trust, the grantor may provide for his or her surviving spouse, and be assured that the balance of the marital trust assets remaining at the surviving spouse's death will pass to the grantor's children. Without the power to appoint assets, the marital trust will also be secure from the claims of a subsequent spouse, if the surviving spouse remarries.

Retirement Plan Assets

In many cases, retirement assets (such as company sponsored pension, profit sharing and 401(k) plans and IRAs) are the most significant marital asset. Special planning is required since retirement plan accumulations are subject to *both* income and estate tax. To achieve the best income and estate tax result, it is normally advisable to name the surviving spouse as the primary beneficiary of retirement benefits payable at death. Only a surviving spouse may roll over the deceased spouse's retirement plan interest (see Chapter 17). Since a "roll over" permits the greatest income tax deferral, naming the surviving spouse as primary beneficiary is often preferred because it achieves the best income tax result. However, doing so may defeat the client's objective of assuring that his or her children receive an interest in the decedent's largest asset. Therefore, choosing a retirement plan beneficiary necessarily involves a tradeoff between the best possible income tax result and assurance that the participant's children will inherit a portion of the retirement plan proceeds.

The nature of qualified retirement plans makes it difficult to solve this problem. Technically, a prospective spouse cannot waive an interest in his or her future spouse's retirement plan.[102] Special language must be inserted into the prenuptial agreement to the effect that the non-participant spouse agrees to waive his or her interest after the marriage when the law recognizes the waiver. Compounding the problem, federal law prevents the naming of a non-spouse as beneficiary of certain retirement plans without the non-participant spouse's consent.[103] Needless to say, planning with retirement benefits requires the assistance of a competent estate planning attorney familiar in such matters.

Michigan Statutory Rights

Michigan statutory rights are designed to protect the economic well being of surviving spouses. A surviving spouse seeking to obtain the benefit of statutory elections must do so in probate court. The following statutory rights accorded to a surviving spouse under Michigan law may be altered or waived with a properly drafted prenuptial or postnuptial agreement:

- The right to receive a family allowance, the amount of which is in the discretion of the probate court[104] (the maximum lump sum available without a court order is $20,000 in 2002);[105]
- The right to receive a homestead allowance in the amount of $17,000 (for 2002; this amount is adjusted annually);[106]
- The right to receive exempt property, such as personal and household items, in the amount of $11,000 (for 2002, this amount is adjusted annually);[107]
- The right to either abide by the terms of the Will of the deceased spouse, or elect to take one-half of the amount he or she would have taken under Michigan law if the deceased spouse had died without a Will (intestate share, See Chapter 5), reduced by one-half the value of the property received by operation of law (i.e. joint ownership, beneficiary designations, etc.), *or*, if the surviving spouse is a woman, elect to take her dower rights (a life estate in one-third of land owned by her late husband);[108]

- The right to control organ donation and disposition of the spouse's body;[109] and
- The right to priority consideration as the deceased's personal representative in an intestate estate.[110]

Conclusion

Second marriage estate planning involves mature discussion between the spouses and their attorney. With the benefit of properly funded separate revocable living trusts, and QTIP marital trusts, spouses should be able to satisfy both the needs of the surviving spouse and of their respective biological children. Prenuptial or postnuptial agreements are advisable where the spouses agree to bypass the survivor and leave their estate directly to their children. All planning must consider the surviving spouse's elective rights under Michigan law.

Chapter 14

What special provisions are available for disabled children?

Parents with disabled children face special estate planning challenges. The cost of supporting disabled children, especially ones with severe disabilities, is typically well beyond the financial means of most parents. They must rely on government programs to at least supplement the care they themselves are able to provide. The death of the disabled child's parents adds to the dilemma: such parents are no longer able to physically care for their child. How to best continue to provide the financial safety net they provided during life is the subject of this Chapter 14.

All but the wealthiest families must rely on government support to care for their disabled children. Supplemental Security Income (SSI),[111] Medicaid,[112] Medicare,[113] and Social Security Disability Insurance (SSDI),[114] though minimal, provide core support to disabled children. Eligibility for all of these programs is conditioned both the child's incompetency as well as financial need.

It is not advisable to leave an outright inheritance to a disabled child. Any inheritance left outright to a disabled child would disqualify the child for government benefits. The child's inheritance would have to be exhausted (to no more than $2,000 in most cases) before the child would again be eligible for government support.[115] The disabled child, having lost his or her inheritance, would be *worse* off than when his or her parents were alive, since the safety net provided by the disabled child's parents would be gone. All that would remain for the disabled child would be poverty level government benefits.

During the 1970's, parents were advised to disinherit their disabled children. Disinheriting a disabled child was thought to be the only way to avoid disqualification from government programs. Unfortunately, this approach exposed disabled children to the harsh realities of government dependency. Another approach was to bequest the disabled child's share to a sibling with the tacit understanding that the inheritance was to be used to support the disabled child. While not disqualifying the disabled child from government benefits, this approach exposed the disabled child's inheritance to a number of contingencies including the death, divorce, bankruptcy or dishonesty of the sibling. Amounts left to the sibling also caused potential estate and income tax complications for the sibling.

The planning device which best addresses the needs of disabled children is known as a Special Needs Trust ("SNT") or "Amenities Trust." These trusts make inherited assets available to a disabled child without disqualifying the disabled child from government benefits. Basically, a SNT directs the trustee to hold and administer trust assets for the benefit of a disabled child with the stated intent that trust income and principal are intended to supplement – rather than replace – government benefits available to the child. Assets held in a properly drafted SNT are not includible as a resource for SSI purposes.[116]

To avoid disqualification, a SNT must provide that: 1) expenditures from the trust are wholly within the discretion of the trustee, and the disabled beneficiary has no right to demand income or principal;[117] and 2) the trust cannot be used to provide items of primary support such as food, clothing or shelter.[118]

Special needs trusts are used to provide specialized medical, optical and dental care, transportation, non-covered medications, travel and entertainment, physical therapy, occupational therapy, electronic equipment, monitoring services and other services not provided under government programs.[119]

It is extremely important that the successor trustee understands his or her duties under the SNT, and properly executes the terms of the trust. As noted above, expenditures from the trust must be within the discretion of the trustee, and the beneficiary may not have the right to demand trust income or principal. A trustee unfamiliar with the government rules may make unintended disqualifying distributions to the disabled child. The trustee should make disbursements directly to the service providers, rather than to the disabled child.

Children wishing to provide for elderly parents should establish a SNT so as to not disqualify parents from Medicaid. As noted in Chapter 19, Medicaid is the government-sponsored program that pays for long term nursing home care. Medicaid eligibility, like programs covering children with special needs, is based on financial need. An outright bequest could unintentionally disqualify a parent from Medicaid. Instead, a SNT should be used to supplement basic Medicaid benefits.

A special needs trust may be established with the proceeds of a lawsuit brought on behalf of the disabled child. If the SNT is created prior to the disabled child's actual or constructive receipt of the lawsuit proceeds, the proceeds will not be considered available for SSI and Medicaid purposes. The balance of a SNT funded with lawsuit proceeds remaining at the child's death, must be used to reimburse SSI or Medicaid for monies expended.[120] By contrast, a SNT created by a parent and funded with assets of the parent's estate may distribute the balance of trust assets remaining at the disabled child's death to beneficiaries of the parent's choosing.

Certainly, the current climate does not suggest that government programs will be expanded to bettercover the disabled. Instead, care must be taken during the estate planning process to provide adequately for disabled children without disqualifying them from available government benefits.

Notes

Chapter 15

When do I need
an irrevocable trust?

Irrevocable trusts are a valuable estate planning tool that are most often used to remove life insurance from estates that would otherwise be taxable. Unlike revocable trusts, which may be amended or revoked at any time during the grantor's lifetime, irrevocable trusts may not be amended or revoked. Also, unlike revocable trusts, the settlor (for clarity, the author uses the term "grantor" when speaking of the sponsor of a revocable living trust, and "settlor" when referring to the sponsor of an irrevocable trust) of an irrevocable trust may never act as trustee, and thus relinquishes full control over both the terms and the administration of the trust.

People who establish irrevocable trusts are not crazy! Quite the contrary, on the advice of counsel, they willingly trade the power to amend, revoke or administer such trusts for exclusion of the irrevocable trust assets from their taxable estate.

Under federal tax law, a decedent's taxable estate consists of assets over which the decedent exercised control at the time of his or her death[121] (see Chapter 2). By relinquishing all such control in an irrevocable trust, the settlor is able to deposit handpicked assets into the irrevocable trust, which then fall outside the grasp of the federal estate tax. To avoid having irrevocable trust assets leech back into the estate of the settlor, the settlor must permanently forego the benefit or use of irrevocable trust assets. The settlor must therefore carefully select assets over which he or she is willing to permanently relinquishing all control or enjoyment.

Irrevocable trusts are most often used by individuals with taxable estates, that is, unmarried individuals with estates exceeding $1,000,000 (2002-2003) and married couples with estates exceeding $2,000,000. Irrevocable trusts, when used as a gifting vehicle, create a sort of limbo or resting area outside the estate of the settlor/donor and the control of the donee. Gifts are made to the irrevocable trust to be held and administered according to the terms of the trust. A donor/parent, for example, with a large estate may begin a substantial gifting program and be assured that the child/donee will not spend the gifted assets until such time as prescribed by the donor/parent.

Life Insurance

Life insurance makes an attractive irrevocable trust asset. The true value of life insurance is not realized until the death of the settlor. Consequently, the fact that a life insurance policy is in trust and outside the control of the settlor during the settlor's lifetime has no real economic impact on the settlor. Owning life insurance in an irrevocable trust also makes good estate tax sense. While insurance proceeds are almost always received by the beneficiary income tax free,[122] they are fully includible in the estate of the insured for federal estate tax purposes.[123] Owning life insurance in an irrevocable trust makes the life insurance tax-free in all respects.

Life insurance provides liquidity to larger estates. Life insurance proceeds are available to satisfy the immediate needs of the decedent's family, such as payment of estate tax, (which is due within nine months of the decedent's death) or to equalize the value of each child's share. As a result, estates consisting primarily of real estate, closely held businesses and other illiquid assets need not sell assets to provide living expenses for the survivor's family or to pay estate tax. An irrevocable trust removes the value of the life insurance proceeds from the decedent's estate so as to not compound the decedent's estate tax liability.

Life insurance is included in the estate of its owner to the extent the owner retains any "incidents of ownership."[124] Incidents of ownership include the right to name or change the beneficiary of the policy, the right to borrow from the policy, or the right to exercise any other right typically possessed by an owner. By relinquishing his or her incidents of ownership in the life insurance policy, the settlor removes the proceeds of the life insurance from his or her estate.

Choice of Insurance

Life insurance policies are like snowflakes; each one is different. Consultation with a qualified life insurance professional is essential to the proper selection of life insurance. Whether to purchase "Term," "Whole

Life," "Universal Life," "Variable Life," "Split Dollar," or some hybrid, depends on the particular needs of the client. Life insurance can insure the life of a single "insured," or can be purchased on joint lives.

A relatively new product called "second to die" or "last to die" insurance has been developed in recent years to address the estate planning needs of married couples. Thanks to the unlimited marital deduction no estate tax is due until the death of the surviving spouse.[125] Consequently, life insurance purchased for the purpose of paying estate tax need not mature until the death of the surviving spouse. Second to die life insurance pays on the death of the second spouse to die. Since the life expectancy of any two spouses will always be longer than the life expectancy of either of the spouses individually, second to die life insurance will always be cheaper than a policy insuring either of the spouses individually.

An irrevocable trust that owns life insurance is sometimes called an Irrevocable Life Insurance Trust ("ILIT"). It is not advisable to fund a newly created ILIT with existing life insurance. A gift of an existing life insurance policy within three years of death will be pulled back into the estate of the decedent, thereby negating the value of the ILIT.[126] Accordingly, unless the settlor is uninsurable, the trustee of the ILIT – once created – should acquire a *new* life insurance policy insuring the life of the settlor. To avoid the three-year rule, the ILIT should be the applicant and initial owner of the new life policy. For this reason, it is important that the ILIT be created as soon as the decision is made to purchase life insurance.

ILIT Funding

To avoid adverse gift tax consequences, strict procedures must be followed when making contributions to an irrevocable trust. As noted in Chapter 9, an individual may make gifts of $11,000 per beneficiary per year without incurring gift tax. To qualify for the gift tax exclusion, gifts must be of a "present interest."[127] For a gift to be of a present interest, the beneficiary must be able to enjoy the gift currently.[128] A transfer to an irrevocable trust is certainly a gift. However, the fact that the beneficiary of a typical ILIT does not receive a benefit until the death of the settlor makes the transfer a gift of a future interest. Fortunately, gifts in trust can be converted from future to present interest transfers by a device known as a "Crummey notice."[129]

A Crummey notice is given to all ILIT beneficiaries contemporaneously with each contribution to the ILIT. The Crummey notice notifies each beneficiary of his or her right to withdraw his or her prorata share of the contribution. Under the terms of the Crummey notice, if such right of withdrawal is not exercised within thirty day of receipt, it lapses. Despite numerous attacks by the IRS, the courts have consistently upheld the validity of Crummey notices.

The following is a sample "Crummey notice".

CRUMMEY NOTICE

Please be advised that a contribution in the amount of $_____ Dollars has been paid over to the _____ Irrevocable Trust dated _____, 2003. You have the right within thirty (30) days of your receipt of this letter to contact _____, the Settlor of the Irrevocable Trust and request that your prorata share of the contribution to the Irrevocable Trust be paid to you. At the expiration of the thirty (30) day period, you will no longer be entitled to make such demand. Should you have any questions, please contact the undersigned.

_____
"Settlor"

Dated: _____

WAIVER OF WITHDRAWAL

I acknowledge receipt of this Crummey Notice. I waive my right to demand withdrawal of this gift from the trust. I do not waive my right to subsequent gifts made to the trust.

Dated: _____

It is the responsibility of the ILIT trustee, as the owner of the life insurance policy, to make annual life insurance premium payments. The settlor should *not* make premium payments directly to the insurance company (bypassing the ILIT), as this could cause inclusion of the proceeds of the policy in the settlor's estate at death. Instead, the settlor should make premium payments to the ILIT. Contemporaneous with the transfer, the settlor (or the trustee of the ILIT) must issue a Crummey notice to each ILIT beneficiary. Only after the 30 day Crummey notice period has lapsed (presumably no beneficiary has elected to withdraw a share of the annual contribution), may the ILIT Trustee make the annual premium payment to the insurance company. (See illustration below)

It is extremely inadvisable to name either the settlor or the settlor's spouse as Trustee of the ILIT. As trustees, the settlor or settlor's spouse would have prohibited powers, causing the life insurance proceeds to be included in their estate. It is common practice, however, to appoint other ILIT beneficiaries such as the settlor's children as trustee.

The procedure for making annual life insurance premium payments is summarized in the following illustration:

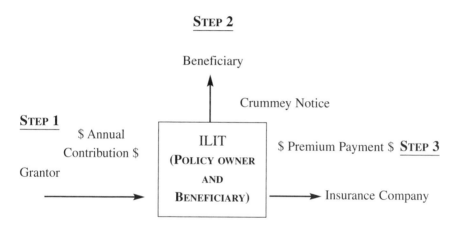

Clients of the author are given the following summary of the procedures to be followed when making annual ILIT premium payments:

PROCEDURE FOR PAYMENT OF LIFE INSURANCE PREMIUMS

Now that you have established an irrevocable trust, it is important that the irrevocable trust be the named *owner* and *beneficiary* of life insurance owned by the trust. The name of your irrevocable trust is the "Harry Barnes Irrevocable Trust dated September 1, 2003, Donna Barnes and Sam Barnes, Trustee." It is also important that you strictly follow the following procedures when making annual life insurance premium payments.

The first step is to establish a checking account in the name of the irrevocable trust. The Trustee of the irrevocable trust, which in your case are Donna and Sam, should have signatory power over the checking account. The tax identification number which was applied for and received from the Internal Revenue Service is 38-1234567, and should be used on the trust's checking account.

Forty-five (45) days prior to the date that an insurance premium is due, a check in the amount of a few dollars more than the amount of the premium should be sent to the trustee of the irrevocable trust. The trustee should immediately deposit the check in the irrevocable trust checking account.

Simultaneous with the transfer of the check to the trustee of the irrevocable trust, the attached Crummey notice should be completed and sent to all beneficiaries of the irrevocable trust. In your case, the beneficiaries of your irrevocable trust are your wife, Wendy and your children, Donna and Sam.

As you will see if you review the Crummey notice, trust beneficiaries have thirty (30) days from the receipt of the notice to demand their pro rata share of the premium payment which has been contributed to the trust. This withdrawal right is intended to comply with the withdrawal privileges outlined in the Crummy (U.S. Supreme Court) case. The withdrawal right creates a present interest transfer to the irrevocable trust and qualifies the transfer for the $11,000 annual gift tax exclusion. It is only after the expiration of the thirty (30) day period that the trustee of the irrevocable trust may pay the life insurance premiums to the life insurance company. You must copy and permanently save all Crummey notices for all years, as the IRS may request copies subsequent to your death.

Should there be several life insurance policies in your irrevocable trust, you should make a single annual contribution to the irrevocable trust in an amount sufficient to pay the premiums on all policies.

It is your responsibility to ensure that the foregoing formalities are observed. Please contact me should you have any questions or require any assistance.

Very truly yours,
ACCETTURA, GROSS & HURWITZ
P. Mark Accettura

Chapter 16

What planning strategies are available for larger estates that contain valuable business or real estate assets?

Whether through outright gift (Chapter 9), transfers in trust (Chapter 15) or charitable transfers (Chapter 18), reducing estate tax involves some sort of gifting. Using the eleven thousand ($11,000) dollar annual gift tax exclusion ($22,000 for married couples), individual "donors" may make substantial annual gifts. If the donor begins a systematic gifting program early enough in life, and has enough beneficiaries to whom gifts can be made, he or she can achieve significant estate tax reduction over time. Not only are the gifted assets removed from the donor and donor's spouse's estate, but the future appreciation of the gifted assets is removed as well.

There are a number of drawbacks to a substantial *outright* gifting program involving cash and liquid assets. First, the donor may not be willing to make substantial outright gifts, fearing that such unrestricted gifts will affect the donee's work ethic. Second, the donor may not have enough liquid assets with which to gift. Finally, the donor may simply not be willing to give up control of his or her assets. Family Limited Partnerships ("FLPs") and Limited Liability Companies ("LLCs") solve most if not all of the problems associated with outright gifts, and consequently have become essential elements in most gifting programs. As an added bonus, substantial gift tax discounts may be available to the donor when valuing the gifted FLP and LLC interests.

Typically, the donor creates a FLP or LLC and transfers business, investment or real estate assets to the partnership or LLC. The donor (often a parent) then *gifts* limited partnership interests and non-managing LLC membership interests to beloved family members (usually children) each year.

The value of the FLP and LLC interests gifted to the children are calculated to closely equal the annual gift tax exclusion ($11,000/$22,000). In some cases, taxable gifts may be advisable (see page 59 "Planning Strategy"). Gifts can be made to the children each year, at the parent's discretion, as long as the parent/donor retains at least a 1% ownership interest in the FLP or LLC.

The general partner of the FLP or the managing member of the LLC retains control over the day-to-day business activities of the entity, making investment and management decisions, and determining when distributions should be made to FLP limited partners or LLC minority members. Naturally, the donor/parent acts as the general partner or managing member of the entity.

FLPs and LLCs facilitate gifts of hard-to-divide assets such as business and real estate interests. Once the FLP or LLC is established, and the business or real estate asset is re-titled into the entity, the donor can readily gift fractional interests of the entity to the beneficiaries. This approach allows the donor to retain his or her cash, as well as control of the gifted assets. It also allows for annual gifting of fractional interests of an illiquid or difficult to divide asset.

Family Limited Partnerships

A Family Limited Partnership ("FLP") is a standard limited partnership with the donor parent acting as the general partner and the donee children owning limited partnership interests. Under Michigan law, a limited partnership must have both a general partner and at least one limited partner.[130] Only general partners are fully liable for partnership recourse debts, while the limited partners are liable for partnership debt only to the extent of their individual investment in the limited partnership.[131] A FLP is not itself a taxable entity.[132] It is said to be a "pass through" entity for the reason that items of income, deduction, gain and loss are calculated at the partnership level and passed directly through to the partners, based on their interest in the partnership, to be taxed at their individual rates.

Limited Liability Companies

A Limited Liability Company ("LLC") is a cross between a corporation and a partnership. It offers the liability protection of a corporation with the pass-through income tax features of a partnership. A LLC is created, owned and managed by its "members." The members, in turn, may elect a managing member or members to manage the day-to-day activities of the LLC.[133] One advantage of a LLC over a FLP is that unlike FLPs, no LLC member is personally liable for the entity's obligations. Remember that the general partner in a FLP remains personally liable for FLP operations.[134] By contrast, all members of a LLC are liable for LLC debts *only to the extent of their investment in the LLC*.[135] Members share in LLC profits and losses based on their ownership percentage. Membership interests in an LLC are considered personal property, as are partnership interests, even if the underlying asset is real property.

Since their introduction into Michigan law in 1995,[136] *LLCs have been the entity of choice*, and in recent years have almost totally replaced limited partnerships. All LLC members may be permitted to manage the company and participate in control of the business without risking loss of limited liability. Under a FLP, at least one general partner must be fully liable for the obligations of the partnership, and the limited partners cannot participate in management without jeopardizing their limited liability.[137]

Family Limited Partnerships and LLCs are preferred over irrevocable trusts as gifting vehicles because they allow the donor to continue to enjoy the benefit of the transferred assets. The donor can also continue to actively manage the assets of the entity. By contrast, the settlor of an irrevocable trust may *neither* retain an interest in the trust nor act as trustee. An irrevocable trust cannot be amended, modified or revoked. Irrevocable trusts, however, due to their ease of formation and administration, remain the preferred technique for excluding life insurance from the donor's estate (see Chapter 15).

Notwithstanding which entity is chosen, both FLPs and LLCs offer flexibility and valuation discount opportunities as well as potential income tax savings. A parent in a higher income tax bracket can give FLP or LLC interests to children in lower income tax brackets. Children will then report their share of income generated by the FLP or LLC at their lower income tax rates.

Parents need not be concerned that the interests gifted to children will be voluntarily or involuntarily transferred to non-family members. Through careful drafting in the FLP agreement or LLC operating agreement, limited partner and LLC member interests are relatively secure against outside creditors. Both the FLP partnership agreement and the LLC operating agreement can prohibit voluntary transfers. Both agreements can severely limit involuntary transfers as a result of the bankruptcy, divorce or insolvency of a partner or member. Such events typically trigger an automatic "buy back" at a nominal price. Buyback may not even be necessary. The inherent lack of marketability of FLP and LLC interests make such interests unattractive to outside creditors. Creditors who acquire limited partner or non-managing member interests become only an assignee, and as such would not be eligible to participate in FLP or LLC management. In divorce, a FLP or LLC interest acquired by gift is considered separate property. In a divorce action, separate property is typically awarded to the owner of the property rather than to the non-owner spouse.

Valuation and Valuation Discounts

Asset valuation is critical in the gifting realm. Naturally, the value of cash and publicly traded securities are easily determined. Closely held business interests and real estate must be determined through written appraisal.

The starting point in valuing gifts of FLP and LLC interests is to determine the value of the assets of the FLP or LLC.[138] The fact that the donee children are receiving a minority interest in an entity, over which they have little control, impacts the value of the gift. A "valuation discount" is applied to gifts of FLP and LLC interests to account for the lack of participation in the management of the entity, as well as the restrictions on transferability of the gifted interest.[139] The law of valuation discounts, as it has developed over the last several years, has consistently recognized that the value of the gifted interests is *less* than the pro-rata value of the underlying FLP or LLC assets.[140] Courts have reasoned that the purchaser of a minority interest would pay less than if the interest was a majority and controlling position.[141] A marketability discount results from the fact that the donee limited partner or member is unable to transfer his or her interest in the FLP or LLC without the consent of the general partner or managing member.[142]

The effect of valuation discounts is that the donor parent can gift a larger FLP or LLC interest to his or her children each year. A thirty-five (35%) discount, for example, would allow the donor parent to make a 35% larger gift within the gift tax exclusion rules. Increasing annual gifting also ensures that a greater percentage of the future appreciation of FLP and LLC assets will be outside the donor parent's estate. If valuation discounts seem too good to be true, someday you may be right. The IRS has indicated that it will attack aggressive valuation discounts especially where the FLP or LLC has been organized for the primary purpose of holding marketable securities. The following is an example of how valuation discounts work:

Harry and Wendy wish to give their children, Donna and Sam, an interest in real property they own together worth $1,100,000. Harry and Wendy create an LLC to which they transfer the real property. Without the benefit of the valuation discount, Harry and Wendy would each retain a 48% interest in the LLC and gift Donna and Sam a 2% membership interest each. The value of their 2% gift is $22,000 (2% x $1.1 M) to each child, all of which is sheltered from gift tax by Harry's and Wendy's annual gift tax exclusions ($11,000 each).

With a 35% valuation discount, H and W can gift $33,846 ($22,000 gift exclusion divided by (1 -.35) = $33,846) annually to each child. Accordingly, H and W would each retain a 46.6154% interest in the LLC after the gift, while each child would have a 3.3846% interest.

The next year, assuming the real property has increased 5% in value to $1,155,000, H and W would agree to amend the LLC operating agreement to give D and S an additional 2.93% (33,846 divided by 1,155,000 = 2.93%) membership interest to each child to reflect an additional $33,846 gift in year 2. The additional gifts would increase D and S interest in the LLC to 6.007% in year 2 thereby reducing H and W's interest in year 2 to 43.993 each.

H and W would follow this procedure annually until they have given away all but one (1%) percent of their interest in the LLC. Each gift is sheltered from tax by H and W's annual gift tax exclusion.

H and W might have gifted an amount in excess of their annual gift tax exclusion (i.e. $11,000/$22,000). Had they elected to do so, they would have reduced their Applicable Exclusion Amount dollar for dollar by the taxable gifts (up to the gift limit of $1,000,000). This can be a very wise approach – even after EGTRRA – where the underlying asset is appreciating rapidly, since a larger percentage of the asset can be gifted before it appreciates. Earlier gifts of a larger percentage of the asset result in a greater percentage of the asset's appreciation being realized by the donee (see "Planning Strategy" at page 59).

The amount of the valuation discount to which the donor is eligible varies depending on a number of factors including:[143]

1) the level of control of limited partners/members;
2) limitations on transfers;
3) levels of partnership/LLC earnings and revenues;
4) the number of partners/members;
5) the nature of the partnership/LLC's underlying assets;
6) the relevant economic environment;
7) the size of the interest being valued; and
8) the specific valuation assignment.

Administration

FLPs and LLCs are separate taxable entities and thus must obtain their own tax identification numbers and file annual federal and state income tax returns (Form 1065 and MI 1065 and SBT). All partners and members must annually include their distributive share of FLP and LLC income and loss (calculated on Schedule K1 of Form 1065) on their personal return. As a practical matter, partners and members must wait to file their personal income tax returns until they have received their K1.

Despite the increased administrative demands of FLPs and LLCs, they are tremendous estate planning tools, which are rapidly gaining in popularity as estate planning tools for larger estates.

Chapter 17

Do tax-preferred retirement plans such as IRA, 401(k), qualified retirement plans, and 403(b) warrant special treatment in estate planning?

Over the last two decades, IRAs, 401(k)s, simplified employee pensions ("SEPs"), and other account-based retirement plans have gained widespread acceptance and popularity. For the most part, they have come to replace traditional employer-provided monthly pension benefit plans. Such account balance plans can easily be transferred from employer plan to employer plan (or to an IRA), and are therefore better suited to our mobile workforce. The move to account-based plans has also shifted the responsibility for retirement savings from the employer to the employee.

The result of the last twenty years of employee-based retirement savings is that IRAs, 401(k)s and other retirement accounts constitute a significant portion of the net worth of most Americans. If you are not eligible for a pension benefit from a previous employer, you might find that, other than Social Security, your retirement accounts are the sole source of your retirement income. Therefore, how you manage, invest, and take distribution from your retirement accounts will be critical to your personal financial security.

At death, retirement accounts pass to the beneficiary named on the account. Federal law requires that qualified pension and profit sharing plan participants (but not IRA, SEP, or 403(b) owners) name their surviving spouse as their primary beneficiary. A beneficiary other than the surviving spouse can be named in such plans only with the written consent of the spouse. Although IRAs, SEP plans, and 403(b) plans do not require that one's spouse be named as primary beneficiary, it is nonetheless common practice for spouses to name each other as beneficiary of such accounts. As beneficiary, several options are available to the surviving spouse. The survivor may:

1. Take a distribution of the entire account and then roll it over into his or her IRA.
2. Leave the money in the deceased spouse's account which the survivor may access as needed.
3. Take a lump sum distribution of the account and elect "10-year averaging".
4. "Disclaim" the interest.

What is appropriate will depend on a number of factors including the size of the deceased participant's retirement accounts, his or her age at the time of death, the survivor's age, and the survivor's need for income. The rules pertaining to retirement account distributions are extremely complex. Although the discussion that follows is difficult, it is of critical importance.

History

Contributions to retirement plans are typically deductible by the employer (or employee) when made.[144] The growth of the contributions is tax deferred until distributed. Recipients of retirement plan distributions are taxed upon the receipt of the distribution at ordinary income tax rates.[145]

The granting of a deduction at the time of the initial contribution, and the deferral of tax on the investment growth of plan assets until their ultimate distribution are in effect tax subsidies by the federal government. In exchange for this subsidy, the Internal Revenue Code requires that retirement plan assets be used during the participant's retirement years.

To discourage pre-retirement use of retirement plan accumulations, a 10% penalty is imposed on withdrawals that occur prior to the participant's[146] attainment of age 59 1/2.[147] To discourage the indefinite postponement of retirement plan distributions (and the resulting income tax), a 50% penalty is imposed on retirement plan distributions which do not at least commence by April 1 following the year in which the participant attains age 70 1/2. A participant's entire interest in the plan need not be distributed at age 70 1/2; it must only begin to be distributed at that age and continue annually over the participant's lifetime (or over the joint lifetimes of the participant and the participant's designated beneficiary) in what are called "required minimum distributions" or "RMDs."[148]

Choosing a Beneficiary

Except in divorce, a participant cannot transfer ownership of his or her retirement plan interests during his or her lifetime, and the beneficiary designation is the mechanism for transferring ownership at death. Generally, it is advisable for the participant to name his or her spouse as the primary beneficiary of retirement benefits. Naming the surviving spouse as primary beneficiary provides the greatest flexibility and allows for the longest and least complex method of deferring income tax in the event of the premature death of the participant. Surviving spouses are given preferred treatment in that only a surviving spouse can "roll over" the deceased spouse's interest in a retirement plan.[149] In other words, upon the death of the participant, the surviving spouse (assuming he or she is the named beneficiary) can take a distribution of the deceased spouse's interest in the plan and within sixty days of the distribution deposit the distribution in the surviving spouse's own IRA. Under this scenario, the surviving spouse can continue to defer income tax on the retirement monies until he or she attains age 70 1/2.

Certain limitations apply in naming a retirement plan beneficiary. Federal law requires that qualified plan participants name their surviving spouse as the primary beneficiary of their interest in the plan.[150] A beneficiary other than the surviving spouse can be named only with the written consent of the spouse. This requirement does not apply to IRAs, SEP plans, 403(b) plans and certain profit sharing plans.

The participant's revocable living trust is the appropriate contingent beneficiary in the event that the participant's spouse (the primary beneficiary) fails to survive the participant. Retirement benefits paid to the revocable living trust will be distributed to the beneficiaries named in the trust. Thus, for example, benefits allocated to a deceased child would automatically be distributed to the children of the deceased child (i.e., grandchild) under the terms of the trust.

ADVANCED PLANNING CAVEAT: A revocable trust should not be named contingent beneficiary where retirement accounts are substantial and there is a wide age difference among trust beneficiaries. The final regulations at Reg. Section 1.401(a)(9)-4, A-5(c) do not permit separate accounts to be established if a trust is the named beneficiary. In such cases, a customized beneficiary designation form should be used to create separate accounts for each trust beneficiary using each separate beneficiary's age to calculate that beneficiaries RMDs.

The "Stretch" Philosophy

For a variety of reasons, it may be very attractive to postpone retirement plan distributions as long as legally possible. First, as a matter of sound income tax planning, it makes sense to recognize taxable income later rather than sooner. Secondly, individuals with large retirement plan assets often have significant alternate sources of income and consequently do not depend on their retirement plans as their primary source of income in retirement. Amazingly, with a little advance planning, the income tax burden of retirement plan distributions can be postponed and spread over the lives of the participant's children and even grandchildren.

In addition to the tax savings, spreading retirement plan distributions over the lives of the participant's children or grandchildren can also provide the trust beneficiaries with a safety net of lifetime income. Affluent parents are often concerned that their children will lose their substantial inheritance through mismanagement, divorce or economic calamity. These same parents are often unwilling to hold their children's inheritance in trust beyond the age of 35 or 40 in the belief that holding assets in trust too long will discourage self-determination and self-reliance. Spreading retirement benefits over children's lifetimes, however, makes such good economic sense that their postponement can be explained to the children not on the basis of the parent's mistrust of their children but on the basis that both parent and children will be economically enriched by the delay.

Rollover

A "roll over" is a distribution of a participant's entire interest in the retirement account (IRA, etc.) that is deposited into a new IRA within sixty days of distribution. Rollovers are tax-free. Only a surviving spouse can roll over a deceased participant's interest. Once rolled, the surviving spouse becomes the owner of the rollover account and therefore is entitled to name a beneficiary of his or her choosing. Of the options available, it is almost always best for a surviving spouse to roll a deceased spouse's IRA, 401(k), or company retirement plan into the survivor's own IRA. Rolling over allows the surviving spouse the greatest investment and distribution flexibility. By rolling over, the surviving spouse is in complete control of the investment house, investment advisor, and investment mix of the new IRA. With his or her own IRA, the survivor will also have a greater ability to defer distributions both during his or her life, and to the survivor's beneficiaries after the survivor's death. The flexibility of the survivor's own IRA is in marked contrast to the option of leaving the deceased spouse's account in his or her former employer's retirement plan. Such plans often offer limited investment options, minimal financial planning advice, and restrictive distribution options. *The only time a survivor should not roll a deceased spouse's account into the survivor's IRA is if the survivor is younger than age 59 1/2 and is in immediate need of the funds.*

Required Minimum Distributions "RMDs"

Retirement distributions may not be deferred indefinitely. You must begin taking annual "required minimum distributions" ("RMDs") when you reach age 70 1/2. You may take your first RMD by April 1 following the calendar year you attain the age of 70 1/2 (the "required beginning date" or "RBD"). Future RMDs must be taken by December 31 of the year in question. Thus, if you wait to take your first distribution until the latest possible time (April 1 of the following year), you will be required to take a double distribution in the second year. To avoid a double RMD, it is advisable to take your first year RMD by December 31 of the year you reach age 70 1/2 rather than waiting until April 1 of the following year.

Example: Mary attains 70 1/2 during 2001 and takes her first RMD March 31, 2002. Mary must take her 2002 RMD by December 31, 2002, resulting in a double RMD distribution in 2002.

RMDs are determined by dividing your retirement plan account balance (as of the previous December 31) by the Applicable Devisor from the Uniform Table below that corresponds to your age. If you have more than one IRA, 403(b), 401(k) or qualified plan, all such plans must be aggregated for purposes of meeting the RMD requirement. Required minimum distributions are just that, minimums. You may always take more than the minimum. Roth IRAs are exempt from the RMD rules.

Example: On December 31, 2001, Mary has $703,285 in her IRA. She is 73 years old. Her RMD for 2002 is $703,285 ÷ 24.7 = $28,473.08.

Rolling Over Versus Not Rolling Over
Distributions at death before required beginning date

If a married participant dies before attaining age 70 1/2, his or her surviving spouse may elect to either roll the deceased participant's interest to his or her own IRA or leave the plan intact. If the survivor chooses the

THE "UNIFORM TABLE"

Table for Determining Applicable Divisor					
Age	Applicable Divisor	Age	Applicable Divisor	Age	Applicable Divisor
70	27.4	86	14.1	102	5.5
71	26.5	87	13.4	103	5.2
72	25.6	88	12.7	104	4.9
73	24.7	89	12.0	105	4.5
74	23.8	90	11.4	106	4.2
75	22.9	91	10.8	107	3.9
76	22.0	92	10.2	108	3.7
77	21.2	93	9.6	109	3.4
78	20.3	94	9.1	110	3.1
79	19.5	95	8.6	111	2.9
80	18.7	96	8.1	112	2.6
81	17.9	97	7.6	113	2.4
82	17.1	98	7.1	114	2.1
83	16.3	99	6.7	115+	1.9
84	15.5	100	6.3	—	—
85	14.8	101	5.9	—	—

rollover option, the survivor's RMDs are based on the *survivor's* age. Thus, if the deceased participant was older than the surviving spouse, rolling over the deceased participant's account will allow the survivor to postpone RMDs until the *survivor's* 70-1/2 year rather than decedent's.

If the survivor decides *not* to roll over, the survivor must begin taking distributions in the year the participant would have attained age 70 1/2. RMDs – where there has been no rollover and where death occurred before the RBD – must be taken under one of the following two methods:

1. Under the "5-year rule" (nothing required to be distributed in the first four years following death, but the entire account must be distributed by December 31st of the fifth year after death); or
2. Annual distributions over the *survivor's* single life expectancy (which is *faster* than the Uniform Table (which calculates minimum distributions on the basis of the joint lives of *two* individuals 10 years apart in age).

If the survivor chooses to roll over, the survivor will begin taking RMDs based on the Uniform Table. At the survivor's death, the survivor's new beneficiaries (for example, the survivor's children) may take the balance of the survivor's interest over *their* life expectancies. By contrast, if the survivor does not roll over, any benefits remaining in the deceased participant's account at the survivor's death must be paid to the contingent beneficiaries *named by deceased participant over the survivor's* remaining life expectancy (which is likely to be substantially shorter than that of the survivor's beneficiaries).

Example: Jim, age 68 and Mary, age 62, are married with two children. Jim has an IRA worth $1,000,000. Jim dies. Mary can:

1. Rollover the entire account into her name. If she rolls over, she does not have to start RMDs until *she* reaches the age of 70 1/2 and she can use the Uniform Table. After her death, the children can take the remaining balance over each of *their* life expectancies, not Mary's;

2. Not rollover the account. If the account is not rolled over, Mary must take the RMD the year *Jim* would have turned 70 1/2. She must either take the entire account within 5 years, or over her single life expectancy. Her life expectancy is figured on a table with shorter lives than the Uniform Table, which uses joint lives. Any balance remaining after Mary's death must be paid out to the children over Mary's remaining life expectancy, not the children's.

Not rolling over might be advantageous if the survivor is substantially younger than 59 1/2 and needs immediate access to the deceased spouse's retirement accounts. *If the survivor rolls over, and takes distributions from the new IRA before the survivor is 59 1/2, the distributions would be subject to a 10% excise tax, in addition to the regular income tax. If the survivor leaves the deceased spouse's account intact, withdrawals are considered to be paid on account of the deceased spouse's death – one of the exceptions to the pre-59 1/2 premature distribution 10% excise tax.*

For example, if the survivor is 52-years-old at spouse's death and elects to roll over the deceased spouse's retirement plan, the survivor could not take a distribution from the rollover IRA without a 10% penalty until the survivor attains age 59 1/2 (a 7 1/2 year wait). By contrast, if the survivor leaves the deceased spouse's account intact, withdrawals may be taken without penalty (they would, however, be subject to income tax), since the distributions are on account of the death of the participant (an exception to the 10% penalty on pre-59 1/2 distributions).

If the surviving spouse is not the designated beneficiary, the deceased spouse's entire account balance must be distributed to the named beneficiary in accordance with either the five-year rule described above, or over the life expectancy of the beneficiary. Under the life expectancy method, distributions must commence no later than the end of the calendar year following the year of the participant's death. If the deceased participant named multiple beneficiaries or a trust, life expectancy is determined based on the life expectancy of the oldest beneficiary or the oldest trust beneficiary. If a trust is named as beneficiary, it is extremely important that a copy of the trust (or a certification of trust that complies with IRS Regulations) be supplied to the Plan Administrator (IRA Custodian) prior to October 31 of the year following the year of death.

Distribution on death after RMDs have begun

The rules for distributions after RMDs have begun (meaning that the deceased participant was at least 70 1/2 at the time of his or her death) are very similar to those for pre-RMD death described above. First, the surviving spouse may roll the deceased spouse's interest over into his or her own IRA. Once rolled, RMDs are based on the survivor's age, not the deceased spouse's. Consequently, if the survivor is younger than 70 1/2, RMDs will cease until the survivor's required beginning date (except that the survivor must take the deceased spouse's RMD for the year of his death). When RMDs do begin, the survivor is eligible to use the Uniform Table. At the survivor's death, the survivor's beneficiaries will be able to take the balance of surviving spouse's account over their life expectancy.

If the survivor does not roll over, distributions during the survivor's life *and* after the survivor's death must be based on the survivor's life expectancy (rather than the longer Uniform Table during the survivor's life and the survivor's children's life expectancy after the survivor's death). Thus, the case for rolling over is even more compelling where death occurs after RMDs have begun. In addition to the extended deferral available to the survivor and the survivor's children, the survivor may be able to discontinue RMDs altogether after the spouse's death if the survivor is not yet 70 1/2.

Post-Death Planning

Whether the participant died before or after his required beginning date, the beneficiary of his retirement accounts is not officially determined until September 30th of the year following the year of his death. This delay allows for significant post mortem distribution planning. In effect, time is allowed to "clean up" a messy beneficiary designation. For example, if the participant named multiple beneficiaries under his retirement account or named his trust as beneficiary, the age of the oldest named beneficiary (or trust beneficiary) must be used for purposes of calculating RMDs. *If one of the multiple beneficiaries is a charity, all beneficiaries must take their distributions in the year following the year of death!*

With proper *post mortem* planning, however, the share of an older beneficiary or a charity can be distributed before September 30th following death (i.e., the "clean up" deadline). In so doing, only the life expectancy of the oldest remaining beneficiaries is counted, lowering RMDs for the remaining beneficiaries. *Also, an older beneficiary can also "disclaim" (essentially give) his or her interest to younger beneficiaries during the clean-up period, eliminating the older beneficiary from the calculation.* Finally, separate accounts may be created for each beneficiary by the end of the year after the year of death. With separate accounts, each beneficiary's RMD is calculated separately based on the age of each such beneficiary.

If a trust is named as beneficiary, a copy of the trust (or a certification of trust that complies with IRS Regulations) must be supplied to the Plan Administrator (IRA Custodian) prior to October 31 of the year following the year of death.

Ten Year Averaging

If the participant was age 50 by January 1, 1986 the survivor should calculate "10-year averaging" on a lump sum distribution of the participant's entire account. Although somewhat radical, this approach can sometimes produce surprising results. Note that 10 year averaging is available only for employer-sponsored qualified retirement plans and not for IRA, SEP, or 403(b) distributions.

Conclusion and Course of Action

Retirement accounts are likely an integral part of your financial security. You should control all aspects of such accounts including investment matters and the timing of distributions. The fact that the accumulations in these accounts are fully taxable for income tax purposes (and estate tax for that matter) dictates that you plan to defer distributions as long into the future as legally possible. Unless a surviving spouse is substantially younger than 59 1/2, he or she should roll the deceased spouse's accounts into the survivor's own IRA. The survivor should name his or her revocable trust as beneficiary of all retirement accounts, or create separate accounts for his or her beneficiaries (see the *Advance Planning Caveat* above). Spreading RMDs over children's lifetimes not only provides maximum income tax deferral, but also provides financial safety for children and perhaps grandchildren.

Obviously, the rules governing retirement plan distribution are incredibly complex. Competent legal and financial advisors employing software programs that illustrate the impact of various planning options should be consulted. Choosing a retirement plan beneficiary is an ominous undertaking. Given that such elections are irrevocable (after death), they cannot be made without a great deal of thought and the input of competent counsel. Based on the foregoing, the following course of action should be taken by participants approaching retirement age:

1. Check current plan beneficiary designations to ensure that they comport with your wishes.
2. Check retirement plan documents to ensure that the distribution strategy chosen is permissible under the plan.
3. Consolidate and merge various plans of like kind (e.g. all IRAs) for simplicity and to ensure that none are overlooked causing the 50% penalty to be imposed.
4. Consider the financial needs of the surviving spouse to determine whether he or she should be named as primary beneficiary.
5. Participants who were age 50 by January 1, 1986 should calculate 10-year averaging on a lump sum distribution. Although somewhat radical, this approach can sometimes produce surprising results. Note that 10 year averaging is available only on employer-sponsored retirement plans and not IRA distributions.
6. Except where the *Advanced Planning Caveat* applies, name a revocable trust as the contingent beneficiary, or, if the participant's spouse is well provided for, as primary retirement plan beneficiary.
7. If a trust is named as beneficiary, the life expectancy of the oldest trust beneficiary is used in calculating RMDs.
8. Stretch out retirement plan distributions as long as legally possible to defer income tax as long as possible.
9. Convert company retirement plans to IRAs prior to age 70 1/2 since IRAs provide greater investment and payout flexibility and are a better vehicle for stretching plan distributions as long as possible. Employer plans shouldn't be converted to IRAs if 10 year averaging is desired

10. Divide large IRAs into separate IRAs to accomplish varied objectives. For example: name second spouse as designated beneficiary on 1/2 and children from first marriage on the other 1/2.
11. Consider conversion to a Roth IRA and avoid the RMD rules entirely.

Michigan Income Tax

Michigan has a flat income tax rate of 4.1% (2002). However, retirement plan distributions are given very favorable income tax treatment. Lump sum distributions are entirely exempt from Michigan income tax. The first $36,090 (2001) of annual retirement plan distributions for single taxpayers and $72,180 (2001) for married filers are tax exempt.

Notes

Chapter 18

What income and estate tax benefits can be derived from charitable transfers?

Charitable transfers generate an income tax deduction if made during life[151] (inter vivos gifts), and are deductible for estate tax purposes when made at death[152] (testamentary transfers). The advantage of inter vivos gifts over testamentary transfers is that they are tax deductible for income tax purposes, and also remove the gifted asset from the donor's estate. Lifetime gifts can substantially reduce the tax bite of high-income taxpayers with large estates. Apart from the obvious tax benefits associated with charitable giving, charitable transfers allow the donor to fulfill his or her "social contract" by subsidizing programs, scholarships and other charitable endeavors that advance the charitable causes of the donor.

There are a myriad of options and gifting vehicles available to anyone who is charitably inclined. Naturally, gifts can be made in cash. Gifts can also be made with appreciated stock, savings bonds, IRAs and other "hot" assets that would result in income tax to the donor if enjoyed during his or her lifetime. Also, Congress, through the Internal Revenue Code, permits and even promotes a wide variety of gifting vehicles discussed in this Chapter 18 that encourage charitable giving. Far from being controversial, the gifting techniques discussed in this Chapter 18 are in fact subsided by the federal government.

A charitable deduction is available for contributions to what are know as "501(c)(3)" organizations;[153] which include churches, educational institutions, foundations and other organizations promoting charitable works. The philosophy behind the deduction (believe it or not, there is actually a philosophy, although a bit foggy, behind the Internal Revenue Code), is that taxpayers should be encouraged to support organizations, causes or services that the government itself would otherwise be forced to provide.

Charitable Split-Interest Trusts

To promote gifting, a number of "split interest" trust options are available. All split interest trusts (discussed in greater detail below) involve the division of the gifted assets into two component parts: income and principal. The most common split interest gifts involve the donor retaining the income from the gifted asset for a period of years or the donor's lifetime with the charity owning the entire asset at the death of the donor; charitable remainder trusts, pooled income funds and charitable gift annuities fall into this category. Charitable lead trusts, by contrast, allow the charity to enjoy the income from the gifted asset for the life of the donor, with the family of the donor owning the gifted asset outright at the death of the donor.

Split interest gifts are a compromise: they allow the donor a current income tax charitable deduction without requiring him or her to forfeit the entire enjoyment of the gifted assets. The donor gives the charity future ownership of the gifted asset and retains the income for a period of years (not exceeding 20) or life. The Code promotes current gifting by allowing both a current charitable deduction and continued limited enjoyment of the gifted asset. The charitable deduction is less than the fair market value of the gift on the date of the gift since the charity cannot immediately enjoy the entire gifted asset. A somewhat complicated calculation of the present value of the future interest must be made to determine the current income tax deduction (see chart on page 113).

Charitable Remainder Trusts

A charitable remainder trust ("CRT") is a tax-exempt trust[154] created during the donor's lifetime. All, or a portion, of the income generated by the property transferred to the CRT is paid to the non-charitable beneficiaries (typically the grantor and/or grantor's spouse) for a term of years (not to exceed 20 years) or for the lifetime of the non-charitable beneficiary. The balance remaining in the CRT at the end of the income term is paid outright to the charitable beneficiary.

A CRT can solve the problem faced by older taxpayers who hold highly appreciated assets. The assets, if sold, would generate a substantial income tax liability. Consequently, to avoid tax, the non-income producing asset is often held in unproductive use. The standard of living of such individuals can be affected if the highly appreciated assets are not income generating. Despite their high net worth, people in this predicament have no spendable income. The CRT itself is exempt from income tax, and thus, can sell highly appreciated property tax-free. After the sale, the *entire* proceeds of the sale (undiminished by income tax) are available to pay an annual income to the donor.

Distributions from the CRT are taxable to the non-charitable beneficiary to the extent that the CRT has income.[155] Like partnership income, the character of the income to the non-charitable beneficiary flows through the CRT. Distributions to the non-charitable beneficiary are first considered ordinary income, then capital gains, then tax-exempt income and finally tax-free return of corpus.[156]

There are two basic forms of charitable remainder trusts: the charitable remainder *annuity trust* ("CRAT") and the charitable remainder *unitrust* ("CRUT").

A charitable remainder annuity trust pays the non-charitable beneficiary a fixed annuity, which is computed either as a fixed dollar amount or as a fixed percentage of the initial value of the trust assets.[157] Whether initially expressed as a dollar figure or as a percentage of the assets, the annual distribution becomes a fixed dollar figure that can never change. The annual distribution must be at least 5% of the initial value of the trust assets and must be paid from principal if income is insufficient.[158] No additional gifts can be made to a charitable remainder annuity trust after its initial funding.[159]

In contrast, a charitable remainder unitrust pays the non-charitable beneficiary an annual payment equal to a percentage (at least 5%) of the value of the trust assets as valued on the first day of the year.[160] An advantage of a CRUT over a CRAT is that it offers greater flexibility. *Additional deductible gifts may be made to a CRUT after its initial funding.* Also, in a CRUT, the annual payment to the non-charitable beneficiary can increase from year to year as the value of trust assets grow.

Recent legislation requires that the charitable remainder interest be at least 10% of the net fair market value of the property as of the date the property is contributed to the CRT.[161] The 10% percent rule when combined with the 5% minimum income rule means that it is impossible to establish a qualified CRT that will last for the lifetime of a beneficiary who is much younger than 25 yeas old.

Individuals with taxable estates typically employ CRTs and the other gifting programs discussed in this Chapter. The first step is for each spouse (if married) to create a revocable trust. This allows the couple to shelter two times the Applicable Exclusion Amount (see Chapter 12). Couples with estates in excess of two times the Applicable Exclusion Amount (2 times $1,000,000 in 2002-2003) have to explore other planning mechanisms to reduce their estate tax liability. They might consider a Family Limited Partnership or LLC (see Chapter 16), or an irrevocable life insurance trust (see Chapter 15). Often, however, because of the size of their estate or the nature of their assets, they are best served by utilizing the split interest gift techniques discussed in this Chapter18.

Example: Assume that Harry (70 years old) and Wendy (60 years old) have a substantial estate. They own highly appreciated non-income producing stock worth $100,000 for which they only paid $5,000. If Harry and Wendy were to sell the stock they would have a $95,000 capital gain. Hearing of the benefits of CRTs, Harry contributes the stock to a CRUT. Harry elects to retain an 8% annual income interest for the balance of his lifetime. Based on tables provide by the IRS, Harry is entitled to a whopping $39,845 charitable income tax deduction (see chart below) in the year the stock is contributed to the CRUT.

The CRT will sell portions of the stock as needed to pay Harry his annual 8% unitrust amount. The sale of the appreciated stock by the CRT is not taxable to the CRT since the CRT is tax exempt. The actual amount received by Harry will be taxable to him as a capital gain since the trust had only capital gains. Note that if the CRT had ordinary income (for example, from stock dividends), the distribution to Harry would first be treated as ordinary income to the extent of the CRT's ordinary income, with the excess treated as capital gains.

The actual dollar figure distributed to Harry will change from year to year depending on the fair market value of the CRT on January 1 of each year.

If Harry and Wendy had decided that they wanted an 8% unitrust income interest for their joint lives, their charitable deduction would have been only $19,335. Since CRTs are irrevocable (except that the charitable beneficiary may be changed) decisions as to the type of trust, the percentage income interest retained, and the duration of the income interest (e.g. single life, joint lives or term of years) cannot be changed once established. The following chart can be used as a guide when deciding the income interest to be retained and the effect on the charitable deduction.

SAMPLE INCOME TAX DEDUCTION ASSUMING $100,000 CONTRIBUTION TO UNITRUST*

Age

		50	60	70	80	70/60 **
Retained	10%	11,405	20,262	33,042	49,860	13,486
Income	9%	13,381	22,938	36,213	53,002	16,106
Interest	8%	15,890	26,159	39,845	56,441	19,335
	7%	19,107	30,062	44,020	60,210	23,332

*   Assumes retained CRUT interest for life of Donor based on ages shown at top of chart.

** Assumes retained CRUT interest for joint life of Donor and Donor's spouse, assuming ages shown.

Pooled Income Funds

Pooled income funds are probably the most common type of split-interest gift.[162] Pooled income funds are created and operated by the charity and closely resemble a mutual fund. Gifts to a pooled income fund are merged with the gifts of other donors. As with CRTs, the donor is entitled to a deduction in the year of contribution that is based on the donor's age and the fund's highest rate of earnings in the previous three years. The donor gives money or property to the fund in exchange for fund units, which entitle the named beneficiary to a ratable share of the fund's actual income each year for life (or, in the case of more than one beneficiary, for a series of joint lives). At the death of the income beneficiary, his or her share of the fund's assets passes outright to the charity.

Charitable Gift Annuities

With a charitable gift annuity, the donor makes a gift to the charity in exchange for a guaranteed income for life. A charitable gift annuity is very much like buying an annuity in the commercial marketplace, except that the donor gets an immediate charitable deduction equal to the excess of the contribution over what the retained annuity is worth, based on IRS tables.

Unlike the pooled income fund, CRUT or CRAT, income from the charitable gift annuity is an obligation of the charity that does not depend on investment results. The rate of return on the gift annuity is not variable, as in a pooled income fund, or negotiable, as in a CRUT or CRAT. As with any annuity, a portion of each year's annuity payment is tax-free, allowing the donor to recover his or her "investment in the contract" over the donor's life expectancy. The simplicity of charitable gift annuities allows for much lower contribution limits; typically in increments of Five Thousand ($5,000) Dollars (depending on the charity). The donor may recognize capital gain if appreciated assets are transferred to the charity to purchase the annuity.

Charitable Lead Trust

A charitable lead trust is a CRT in reverse: The charitable beneficiary is entitled to the current *income* with the non-charitable beneficiary entitled to the remainder.[163] The general rules of CRT's apply to charitable lead trusts with the exception that there is no requirement that the payout rate be a minimum of 5%.[164] Charitable lead trusts are primarily used to save estate and gift taxes, and do not provide the same income tax saving opportunities as CRTs. To accomplish this result, the grantor must postpone the receipt of the trust assets by his family until the charitable lead interest of the charity has expired.

NIMCRUT

A NIMCRUT is a "net income" CRUT with "make up" provisions.[165] Such trusts annually distribute the *lesser* of trust net income and the unitrust percentage. For example, if the donor elected an 8% unitrust amount, but the NIMCRUT earned only 4% for the year, the donor would receive only a 4% distribution. Distributions in years where the net income is less than the unitrust percentage can be made up in later years to the extent that income in the future year *exceeds* the unitrust amount. NIMCRUTS are a useful tool for high net worth individuals who are still working. They receive a charitable deduction in the year of creation when their income is high, and defer income to retirement years when they are in a lower tax bracket. Income can be manipulated during the donor's working years by investing in non-income producing assets such as growth stocks and deferred variable annuities. At retirement, the trustee would switch trust investments to high-yield investments producing substantial returns. Because of their resemblance to traditional retirement plans these arrangements are sometimes called "retirement unitrusts" or "charitable IRAs."

Wealth Replacement Trusts

A potential obstacle to charitable giving is the fact that gifted assets do not pass to the next generation. It is the author's observation that despite the bravado reflected on bumper stickers: "I'm spending my children's inheritance," parents really *do* want their children to receive their inheritance. Fortunately, the needs of the family can be accomplished by creating a "wealth replacement trust" concurrently with the split interest trust.

A portion of the income distributed to the donor from the CRT can be used to purchase a life insurance policy inside an irrevocable trust (called a "wealth replacement trust"). This approach allows for a substantially larger *tax-free* inheritance to the next generation. While assets would have been fully taxable if not contributed to the charitable entity, they pass tax free from the wealth replacement trust. The donor gets a substantial current income tax deduction and annual unitrust income while leaving an estate tax free inheritance. Use of a CRT in combination with a wealth replacement trust is illustrated below:

CHARITABLE GIVING AND WEALTH REPLACEMENT

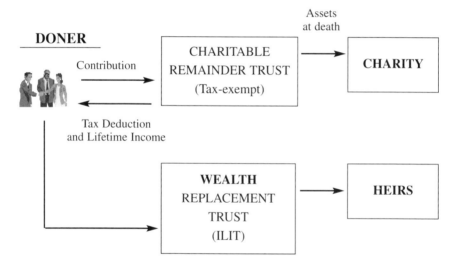

Income Tax Deduction Limits

The extent to which charitable contributions can be deducted for income tax purposes depends on a number of factors including the type of charity, and the type of property being contributed. Charitable bequests (i.e., transfers at death), by contrast, are 100% deductible.

The status of the charitable beneficiary affects the deductibility of the charitable contribution. Basically, a charity can be either a 50% charity or a 30% charity. Fifty (50%) percent charities are called "public" charities and include churches, educational institutions, hospitals and governmental units.[166] Thirty (30%) percent charities include "private" foundations which are often identified by the name of the benefactor.[167] The Ford Foundation and Kresge Foundation are examples of private foundations. Charitable contributions to public charities are deductible up to a maximum of 50% of the donor's adjusted gross income ("AGI"), while contributions to private foundations are deductible up to a maximum of 30% of the donor's AGI.[168] Contributions in excess of the 50%/30% ceilings may be carried over and deducted up to five years *after* the year of contribution.

The nature of contributed property also affects the charitable contribution deduction. Gifts of cash and property that is not long-term capital gain property (ordinary income or short-term gain) are deductible up to 50% of AGI.[169] Gifts of long-term capital gain property are deductible up to 30% of AGI, subject to the overall 50% ceiling.[170] Contributions in excess of the 50%/30% ceilings may be carried over and deducted for up to five future years.[171] Gifts to private foundations (30% charities) are deductible up to 30% of a donor's AGI, with a five-year carryover, except for long-term capital gain property, which is subject to a 20% ceiling. The deduction is reduced to basis if property is not marketable securities contributed after June 30, 1998.[172]

Chapter 19

Do I have to exhaust my assets before Medicaid will pay my nursing home costs?

The general aging of our population[173] along with advances in medical science have greatly increased the likelihood that we will live beyond the point that we can care for ourselves. The delivery of long term care to the elderly has evolved to include various forms of home care and long term nursing home care, all of which are very expensive. Long term care (LTC) ranges from help with day-to-day activities in the home (such as bathing, dressing, preparing meals, etc.), to more sophisticated services such as skilled nursing care. While typical health care services are cure oriented, long-term care involves treatment of chronic conditions and thus is said to be care oriented. Long term care can be provided in one's own home, an adult day care setting, in an assisted living/residential care facility, or a skilled nursing care facility.

The greatest concern for older Americans is that their entire wealth accumulation will be dissipated if they experience an extended stay in a skilled nursing care facility. According to a recent report, the average cost of a year in a nursing home was approximately $54,000 in 1997, roughly equating to $150 per day.[174] Further, according to the New England Journal of Medicine, more than 50% of those who require 24-hour care will need such care for more than one year. On average, that group will need care for 2 1/2 years.

The high cost of skilled nursing care is of special concern to "community spouses," that is, the non-institutionalized spouse of a skilled nursing care patient. This Chapter 19 focuses on the sources of funding for the payment of LTC; those being: 1) Medicare; 2) private pay (including long term care insurance for those eligible and able to provide their own); and finally 3) Medicaid.

Medicare

Medicare covers LTC only under limited circumstances, and only for a limited period of time. Medicare will reimburse the cost of a stay in an approved skilled nursing facility that immediately follows a three-day or more hospital stay.[175] Further, to be eligible, you must enter the skilled nursing facility within 30 days of your discharge from the hospital, and the skilled nursing facility stay must be for the same reason as the hospitalization.[176]

Medicare only covers the first 100 days of the skilled nursing care stay, covering 100% percent of the cost of the first 20 days, and only the cost of the remaining 80 days to the extent that the cost *exceeds* $99.00.[177] Slightly augmented coverage may be provided under private "medigap" coverage during the 100-day period, but medigap coverage does not otherwise cover LTC.

The cost of LTC, after Medicare benefits are exhausted (if eligible at all), falls to the patient. The likelihood that you will private-pay is high, considering that Medicare paid only 10.6% of skilled nursing home cost in 1994. The patient will continue to be required to pay the cost of his or her own LTC until his or her assets are sufficiently exhausted to be eligible for Medicaid. Individuals with adequate means and who enjoy reasonably good health may insure against this potentiality by purchasing long term care insurance.

Summary of Medicare Skilled Nursing Facility Coverage

Benefit	Medicare Pays	You Pay
First 20 days of Care	100% of Approved Amount	None of approved amount, but all of non-approved amount
Next 80 days of care	Only above $99.00 a day	Up to $99.00 a day
Beyond 100 days	Nothing	All Costs

Private Pay

The cost of LTC, after Medicare benefits have been exhausted (if eligible at all), falls to the patient. The patient will continue to be obligated to pay the cost of his or her own LTC until his or her assets are sufficiently exhausted to be eligible for Medicaid. Individuals with adequate means and who enjoy reasonably good health may insure against this potentiality by purchasing long term care insurance. Perhaps to compensate for reductions in Medicaid, Congress in The Health Insurance Portability and Accountability Act of 1996,[178] provided new tax incentives to owners of private long term care insurance. Qualified premium payments are now considered as medical expenses and are therefore deductible to the extent that when added to other medical expenses they exceed 7.5% of adjusted gross income.[179] Under the 1996 Act, benefit payments from the long-term care insurance policy are income tax free.[180] For those able to afford it, the new legislation has made long term care insurance an attractive method of insuring long term, quality care.

Medicaid

Medicaid is a federally funded, state-administered welfare program restricted to the financially indigent. Accordingly, to qualify for Medicaid the patient must have exhausted substantially all of his or her non-exempt assets. Individuals may be tempted to gift their assets to family members in order to qualify for Medicaid. This process, called "divestment," can be perilous. The Balanced Budget Act of 1997[181] makes it a criminal act for a professional advisor to counsel a client to dispose of assets in order to qualify for Medicaid. Secondly, the better skilled the nursing home facility, the less likely it is that they will accept Medicaid patients. Some facilities are entirely private-pay, accepting no Medicaid patients. Others limit the number of Medicaid beds available, giving priority to private pay patients. In light of the national shortage of skilled nursing care facilities and beds, patients attempting entry as Medicaid patients may land at the most undesirable facilities.

The following is a thumbnail sketch of the Medicaid eligibility rules as they apply to long-term nursing home care. For ease of discussion, the individual applying for Medicaid will be called the "Applicant."

An individual will be eligible for Medicaid only if he or she is at least age 65, demonstrates financial need, and follows the procedures for applying for Medicaid. With respect to financial need, the Applicant may have no more than $2,000 of assets and *limited* income. Counted assets include all assets including IRAs, the cash value of life insurance, stocks, and savings bonds. Assets owned in the Applicant and Applicant's spouse's name are counted as entirely owned by the Applicant, as are assets held in a revocable trust. *However*, the following assets (sometimes referred to as "excluded assets") are *not* considered for purposes of the $2,000 limit:[182]

1. An automobile of any value;
2. The Applicant's principal residence of any value ("homestead");
3. Household goods, furniture and personal affects, including clothing and jewelry;
4. A prepaid irrevocable funeral contract;
5. Cemetery plot;
6. Cash value of life insurance up to $1,500;
7. Income producing real property where the income derived from rents is at least 6% of the Applicant's equity in the rented property; and
8. Miscellaneous other exemptions not relevant here.

If medical expenses exceed income, then the income test is met. Medicaid will pay medical expenses to the extent they exceed income. Income is defined as both earned and unearned income including interest, dividends, rents, social security benefits and retirement benefits.

Clients often ask: "How does the State know what we have?" The simple answer to this question is that under the penalty of perjury the Applicant must file an Asset Declaration Form (FIA-4574-B) attached as Exhibit B, and provide independent verification of the ownership and value of each asset and source of income.

Two of the most misunderstood and complicated aspects of Medicaid eligibility are the divestment and spousal impoverishment rules.

Divestment

Divestment is the transfer of countable (i.e., non-excluded) assets for less than fair market value within sixty (60) months of applying for Medicaid nursing home benefits for transfers to or from a trust, and thirty-six (36) months for all other transfers. It is important to understand that divestment does not occur if countable assets are converted to exempt assets of equal value. For example, paying off the mortgage on your home, buying a new car or purchasing an irrevocable funeral arrangement do not constitute divestment. The period of disqualification on account of divestment is measured by dividing the "uncompensated value" of the transferred assets by the average monthly private paid nursing home costs of the particular nursing home facility applied for. For example, if on the eve of entering a nursing home and applying for Medicaid, Wendy gives her son, Sam, $120,000, Wendy will be ineligible for Medicaid for twenty-five (25) months ($120,000 divided by the average monthly cost of long term care in Michigan ($4,703 in 2002[183]).[184] There is no limit on the length of disqualification resulting from divestment.[185] Finally, a rule that appears to have no logical basis on its face is that transfer of the Applicant's homestead within the thirty-six (36) month period, unless the transfer is to the spouse or a disabled child of the Applicant, is considered a divestment (despite the fact that the asset is an exempt asset). A transfer of the Applicant's homestead to a revocable living trust is considered a divestment.[186] Transfers of other exempt assets within the thirty-six (36) month period are not considered to be divestments.

Spousal Impoverishment Rules

Spousal Impoverishment Rules were enacted in 1988 as part of the Medicare Catastrophic Coverage Act. In order to prevent the economic devastation of the community spouse (a term used to describe the non-institutionalized spouse), the Spousal Impoverishment Rules treat the assets and income of the husband and wife as part of a common pot with the community spouse entitled to a guaranteed share. First, with respect to income, the community spouse's income may be supplemented from income of the resident spouse up to a minimum of $1,493 and a maximum of $2,232 per month in 2002. The community spouse is also entitled to one-half (1/2) of the countable assets (in addition to all of the excluded assets) not to exceed $89,280 but with a guaranteed minimum of $17,856. These values are indexed for inflation. The Spousal Impoverishment Rules are an important development and allow retention of a much greater amount of assets by the community spouse.

Estate Recovery

As part of 1993 federal Legislation,[187] Michigan is required to establish an estate recovery program to seek reimbursement of the Medicaid benefits paid on behalf of the decedent from the estate of a deceased Medicaid recipient. For purposes of the Act, "estate" may be defined as the decedent's probate estate, or all assets of the decedent, including jointly held property and property owned by the decedent's living trust. The estate recovery program was effective October 1, 1993. However, as of this writing, Michigan is the *only state in the country* that has not implemented an estate recovery program.

Planning Techniques and Strategies

There are several steps that can be taken to preserve the estate of someone needing long term nursing home care:

1. Purchase long term care insurance to cover the exigency of long term care.
2. Hold on to your exempt assets, especially the principal home.
3. Convert counted assets into exempt assets. Examples include paying down the mortgage on the home, improving the home, or acquiring a more expensive home.
4. Since the 6% income rule does not apply to homesteads, the homestead can be rented to family members for a very modest amount while the Applicant is in the nursing home. Family members could in turn re-rent the property at the current fair market value rent. This arrangement would prevent all of the rental income from being treated as income eligible for nursing home care payment.
5. Investment real estate could be acquired (even a common tenancy in a family member's residence would qualify) as long as the 6% income to equity ratio is met.
6. Outright gifts and gifts to an irrevocable or testamentary trust provide the greatest planning opportunity. Outright transfers more than thirty-six (36) months from the month in which application for Medicaid is made, or trusts more than sixty (60) months prior to such date are not counted for purposes of Medicaid eligibility. Use of trusts avoids an outright transfer of assets to family members who may dispose of the assets in a fashion unacceptable to the Applicant.
7. Consider monthly gifts in what has come to be known as "serial divestment." This technique involves monthly gifts in an amount that is less than the average monthly nursing home cost, as determined by the state. For example, if the average monthly nursing home cost is $4,703 (2002), a gift of $4,702 results in *no* disqualification, since Michigan does not recognize partial period disqualifications and always rounds down to the next whole number of months. Since each month is a new time period for computing gifts, $4,702 could be gifted *each* month with no disqualification. A gift of $9,404 would result in only one month of disqualification even though the divestment was 1.99 times the monthly amount. Serial divestment depends on two quirks in the law: first, that each month must be treated as a new gifting period, and second, that there be no

partial period disqualification for gifts of less than the average monthly nursing home cost. Applicants should consult with an attorney familiar in such matters to determine if there have been any changes in the law that affect serial divestment.

8. Purchase an actuarially sound annuity ("ASA"). An ASA is a commercially available or private annuity that does not guarantee a period longer than the life expectancy of the Applicant.

The rules discussed herein apply specifically to Michigan. The Medicaid rules change frequently. Therefore, any planning strategy must be reviewed in light of current and future law changes. Each client's strategy will also depend on his or her particular situation.

Notes

Chapter 20

My children are well off. Can I leave my estate to my grandchildren?

Transfers during life or at death to a "skip person" may be subject to the generation skipping transfer tax ("GST"). A transfer to a grandchild while their parent is still alive is considered a direct skip, and is subject to the GST. The philosophy behind the GST is that each generation should be subject to estate tax. Transfers that skip a generation are therefore subject to a tax that is at least as severe as the estate tax.

The GST is an onerous, flat, fifty-five (55%) percent tax that is imposed in addition to the regular gift and estate tax. A skip person is defined as a person in a generation that is two or more generations below the transferor.[188] Thus, grandchildren of the transferor are skip persons. However, a transfer to the children of a deceased child will not be considered to be a generation skipping transfer. Grandchildren who are the children of a deceased child of the transferor move up a generation, and are therefore not considered skip persons.

Example: Harry is a successful business owner who wants to establish a trust for his two grandchildren, Greg and Gretchen, whose father, Sam, was killed in an automobile accident. Harry funds each trust with $1 million of securities. The GST will not apply to the transfers because Greg and Gretchen's father was dead when the trust was originally established.

Fortunately, all individuals are allowed a $1million dollar exemption ($1,060,000 indexed for inflation) from the GST.[189] In addition, direct skip transfers that are within the $11,000 gift tax exclusion, and gifts that qualify for tuition and medical expenses (see Chapter 9) are not subject to the GST. Thus, a grandparent can make annual gifts of $11,000 per grandchild, plus a total of $1 million dollars in additional generation skipping transfers to grandchildren during life or at death GST free.

Gifts in trust that qualify for the gift tax exclusion rarely qualify for the GST exclusion. For gift tax purposes, gifts in trust qualify as present interest gifts by virtue of the Crummey power (see Chapter 15). Gifts in trust will qualify for the GST exclusion only if: (1) no part of trust income or corpus can be distributed to anyone other than the trust beneficiary during the beneficiary's life, and (2) trust assets are included in the beneficiary's gross estate if the beneficiary dies before the trust terminates.[190] To qualify for the GST exclusion, a trust would have to benefit a single skip person, and would have to grant a general power of appointment to the beneficiary in the event the beneficiary predeceased the grandparent.

The GST applies to "direct skips", "taxable trust distributions", and "taxable trust terminations." A direct skip is a transfer of property, subject to either the estate or gift tax, to a skip person.[191] A taxable distribution is any distribution (other than a taxable termination or a direct skip) from a trust to a skip person.[192] A taxable termination is the termination of the interest of a beneficiary in a trust if immediately after the termination, no non-skip person has an interest in the trust and future distributions can only be made to a skip person.[193]

Example: If Grandmother creates a trust for the lifetime benefit of her children, and then her grandchildren upon the death of her last surviving child, a taxable termination occurs on the death of her last surviving child.

The GST is incredibly complex! Only estate planning professionals with extensive experience can be expected to understand the rules. Unfortunately, the GST cannot be ignored. Inadvertent generation skipping transfers can occur where children of the decedent die between the deaths of their parents (see below). GST planning primarily involves proper allocation of the $1 million dollar GST exemption to transferred property. Revocable living trusts must accommodate the proper allocation of the GST exemption. To maximize the GST exemptions, revocable living trusts segregate trust assets on the basis of those that are subject to GST ("non-exempt" assets) and those which are exempt ("exempt" assets). Clients are confused by the numerous references to the GST in their revocable living trust document, sometimes uttering aloud "I'm not leaving a million dollars to my grandchildren." This Chapter 20 attempts to explain the reason why GST provisions must be addressed in every revocable living trust.

Trusts for Children

Trusts commonly hold funds for the benefit of children until they are old enough to manage an outright distribution. Such trusts create a generation skipping transfer if, at the child's death, before the termination of the trust, the trust funds pass to the child's descendants.

> **Example:** Harry creates a trust for the benefit of his son, Sam. In the event that Sam is not age 35 at Harry's death, the Trust provides that trust assets will be held and used for Sam until he attains age 35, at which time the balance of the trust assets will be distributed to Sam outright. The trust further provides that in the event that Sam dies after Harry but before attaining age 35, his share passes to his children. If Sam survives Harry but fails to live to age 35, the share that passes to Sam's children is considered generation skipping transfer.

Another common trust provision that can result in a generation skipping transfer is a transfer in trust for the grantor's spouse followed by an outright transfer to the grantor's children at the spouse's death. Such trusts usually provide that in the event a child of grantor predeceases grantor or grantor's spouse, the share of such child passes to the deceased child's issue. A transfer to grandchildren resulting from the death of child who dies after one parent but before the other is a generation skipping transfer.

> **Example:** Harry dies leaving assets in a revocable living trust for the benefit of wife, Wendy, to be used for her benefit for the balance of her lifetime. At Wendy's death, trust assets are to be distributed to Harry's children, Sam and Donna, or the issue of a child who fails to survive Wendy. If Donna survives Harry, but predeceases Wendy, the share that passes to Donna's children is a generation skipping transfer.

Transferor

Identifying the transferor of a generation skipping transfer is important because only the transferor or the transferor's executor may allocate the GST exemption.[194] The transferor is the donor for any transferred property subject to the gift tax and is the decedent for transfers of property subject to estate tax.[195] Transfers that qualify for the marital deduction cause the transferred property to be subject to gift or estate tax on subsequent transfers by the recipient spouse. The recipient spouse becomes the transferor when property is later included in the estate of the recipient spouse.

Example: At Harry's death, his revocable living trust divides into a family and marital trust (see diagram page 70). Harry is the transferor of the family trust because funding of the family trust is a taxable transfer (even though it is offset by Harry's unified credit). Wife, Wendy, is the transferor of the marital trust since the balance of the marital trust remaining at Wendy's death is included in her estate and therefore taxable to her (see Chapter10). Harry can use all of his GST exemption.

Reverse QTIP Election

A special election is available to Harry's executor in the above example if the marital trust is a QTIP trust. Harry's executor may make a "reverse QTIP election,"[196] which has the effect of treating the marital Trust (for GST purposes only) as if no QTIP election was made. The reverse QTIP election effectively treats Harry as the transferor, allowing him to allocate his full $1 million dollar GST exemption. The reverse QTIP election is made on the gift tax return (Form 709) or estate tax return (Form 706).

Early GST Exemption Allocation

The benefit of the $1 million dollar GST exemption can be maximized if used during the life of the transferor. The future appreciation of assets to which GST has been allocated is not subject to the GST.

Example: In 1999, Harry transferred $500,000 of stock to a trust for the benefit of his son, Sam, for his life, then to Harry's grandchildren. One half of Harry's GST exemption was timely allocated to the transfer on Form 709. The stock is worth $4 million dollars at Sam's death, when it passes to Harry's grandchildren. No GST is due on what would otherwise be a taxable termination since the GST exemption was allocated when the gift was made. Thus, once the exemption is allocated, any further generation skipping transfers of the exempted property remain exempt from the GST tax.

Married couples can maximize their separate $1 Million dollar GST exemptions by dividing their assets to ensure that each spouse has a revocable living trust funded with at least $1 million dollars. Further, a husband and wife may elect to split a gift, allowing the gift to be deemed to have been made one-half by each spouse. For GST purposes, each spouse is treated as the transferor of one-half of the gift, and each spouse may allocate his or her GST exemption to their respective gift.[197]

Use of Multiple Trusts to Optimize the GST Exemption

Separate trusts inside a single revocable living trust allow the successor trustee to segregate assets that are subject to the GST from those that are not. Once separated, the GST exemption can be allocated between the trusts in such a way as to maximize the exemption. The GST exemption will be allocated to the non-exempt trust for the benefit of a skip person, while no such allocation is necessary for the exempt trust benefiting non-skip persons, since such transfers are not subject to the GST. In the parlance of the GST, the separate trusts should have an inclusion ratio of either "0" or "1." The trust with the inclusion ratio of 0 is used to provide benefits only for skip persons while the trust with the inclusion ratio of 1 is used to provide benefits for non-skip persons. Absent the segregation of assets described above, the GST exemption would be allocated to all trust assets on a pro rata basis. A trust with assets in excess of $1 million dollars would have an inclusion ratio between 0 and 1. The GST exemption would then be wasted on a distribution to a non-skip person since unprotected assets could have been distributed to a non-skip person without GST tax consequence anyway.

The Inclusion Ratio

The inclusion ratio is the fraction used to determine the GST tax rate applicable to a GST transfer.[198] An inclusion ratio of 0 will result in no GST, while an inclusion ratio of 1 results in a full 55% GST. The inclusion ratio is 1 minus the applicable fraction.[199] The numerator of the applicable fraction is the amount of the GST exemption allocated to the trust or transferred property. The denominator of the applicable fraction is the final gift or estate tax value of the property transferred.

> **Example:** Harry transfers $6 Million dollars to a trust he establishes for his grandchildren. Harry allocates his entire GST exemption to the trust on a timely filed Form 709. The applicable fraction is $1 million divided by $6 million, or .167 (rounded to the nearest thousandth). The inclusion ratio is .833 (1 - .167). Any taxable transfer with respect to the trust will be taxed at 83.3% of the GST tax rate of 55% (e.g., 55% times 83.3% = 45.21%).

EGTRRA

In its current form, EGTRRA would repeal the GST effective in the year 2010.

End Notes

1   The Applicable Exemption Amount is $1,000,000 in 2002.
2   See the Grantor Trust Rules contained in Sections 671 through 679 of the Internal Revenue Code. All references to "Code" or "Internal Revenue Code" are to the Internal Revenue Code of 1986, as amended.
3   Public Act 386 of 1998.
4   The term "Gross Estate" is defined in Section 2031.
5   Defined in Section 2051(a).
6   IRC Section 2033.
7   IRC Section 2042.
8   IRC Section 2039.
9   IRC Section 691.
10   IRC Section 2040.
11   IRC Section 2040(a).
12   IRC Section 1014.
13   IRC Section 2035(d).
14   IRC Section 2036.
15   IRC Section 2038.
16   IRC Section 2041(a)(2).
17   IRC Section 2032A.
18   IRC Section 2032.
19   Private Letter Ruling 94-10028.
20   The Patient's Rights Act, MCLA 700.5506 et. seq. All 50 states now have legislation authorizing either living wills, advance directives and health proxies.
21   MCLA 700.5508.
22   Journal of the American Medical Association, November 22, 1995. The study concluded that only approximately fifty percent (50%) of all patients who requested not to be resuscitated actually had their preferences honored.
23   MCLA 700.2501.
24   MCLA 700.2502.
25   MCLA 700.2101 et. seq.
26   MCLA 700.2102
27   MCLA 700.2103.
28   MCLA 700.2106.

29   MCLA 700.2102.
30   MCLA 700.2102.
31   MCLA 700.2103.
32   MCLA 700.2102.
33   MCLA 700.1210.
34   MCLA 700.2103.
35   MCLA 700.2106.
36   MCLA 700.2103.
37   MCLA 700.2103.
38   MCLA 700.2106.
39   MCLA 700.2103.
40   Block v Schmidt, 296 Mich 610, 296 NW 698 (1941)
41   Norris v. Hall, 124 Mich 170, 82 NW 832 (1900).
42   Lilly v. Schmock, 297 Michigan 513, 298 NW 116 (1941).
43   MCLA Section 451.475
44   Guilds v. Monroe County Bank, 41 Mich App 616, 200 NW2d 769 (1972).
45   MCLA Section 451.471 et. seq.
46   M.C.L.554.521, et. seq.
47   MCLA 3308.
48   MCL 700.3705,.3306,.3801
49   MCL 700.3801.
50   MCL 700.3801.
51   MCL 700.3803.
52   MCL 700.3301.
53   MCL 700.3982
54   IRC Section 2503(b).
55   IRC Section 2503(b)(2).
56   IRC Section 2513.
57   IRC Section 2503(e).
58   IRC Section 2523.
59   IRC Section 2523(f).
60   IRC Section 25123(i)(2).
61   IRC Section 2503(c).
62   Reg. 25.2503-4(6).
63   See IRC Section 7520.
64   IRC Section 2702.
65   Section 2702(a)(3)(A)(iii).
66   The gift tax marital deduction is authorized under IRC Section 2523(a) and the estate tax marital deduction under IRC Section 2056.
67   IRC Section 2056(b).
68   IRC Section 2056(b)(7). The decedent's Personal Representative must elect QTIP status on Schedule M of Form 706.
69   IRC Section 2056(d).
70   IRC Section 2041(a)(2).

71 IRC Section 2044.
72 IRC Section 2201A.
72.1 IRC Section 103.
73 IRC Section 691.
74 IRC Section 101(a).
75 Annuities (IRC Section 1014(b)(9)(A) and income in respect of a decedent (IRC Section 1014(c)) items (described later in this Chp. 17) do not receive a stepped-up basis.
76 IRC Section 1014.
77 IRC Section 1012.
78 IRC Section 1016.
79 IRC Section 1014(a).
80 Id.
81 Id.
82 Id.
83 IRC Section 2032(a)(2).
84 IRC Section 1014(e).
85 IRC Section 691.
86 Treasury Regulation 1.691(a)-1(b).
87 IRC Section 691(c).
88 Treasury Regulations 1.691 (a)-4(a).
89 IRC Section 2056(a).
90 IRC Section 2056(a).
91 MCL 205.232(1).
92 The Michigan Estate Tax is equal to the Credit for State Death Taxes allowed under IRC Section 2011(b).
93 New IRC Section 2001(c).
94 New IRC Section 2033A.
95 Michigan Rules of Professional Conduct (MRPC) 1.7.
96 Id.
97 In re Benker Estate 416 Mich 681 (1982).
98 MCLA 557.28; MCLA 700.2205; Rinveldt v. Rinveldt, 190 Mich App 372; 475 NW 2d 478 (1991).
99 Rinveldt v Rinveldt, Supra.
100 MCLA 552.401
101 MCLA 700.2202; Soltis v First of America Bank – Muskegon, 203 Mich App 435 (1994).
102 Retirement Equity Act of 1984.
103 Retirement Equity Act of 1984.
104 MCLA 700.2403.
105 MCLA 700.2405.
106 MCLA 700.2402.
107 MCLA 700.2404.
108 MCLA 700.2202.
109 MCLA 333.10102; MCLA 333.10108.

110 MCLA 700.3203.

111 42 USC 1381 st.seq.

112 42 USC 1396 st. seq.; MCLA 400.105 et. seq.

113 42 USC 1395 et. seq.

114 42 USC 401 et. seq.

115 Program Eligibility Manual, 400; 42 USC 1382(a); 20 CFR 416.1205(a) – (6).

116 Miller v. Department of Mental Health, 432 Mich 426 (1989).

117 Id.

118 See Program Operations manuals System (POMS) and Michigan Department of Social Services, Program Eligibility Manual (PEM)

119 Joel S. Welber, "The Use of Trusts of Complement Essential Governmental Benefits in Residential-Life Care Planning", Michigan Bar Journal, May 1996.

120 Mary T. Schmitt Smith, Esq., "A Primer on Interceptor or Special Needs Trusts." MTLA Quarterly, Winter 1997.

121 IRC Sections 2036 and 2038.

122 Section 101(a).

123 Section 2042.

124 Section 2042(2).

125 Section 2056(a).

126 Section 2035(b).

127 Section 2503(b).

128 Treasury Reg. Section 25.2503-3(b) "An unrestricted right to the immediate use, possession, or enjoyment of property or the income from property (such as a life estate or term certain) is a present interest in property."

129 Crummey powers derive their nam from the Ninth Federal Circuit Court Case of Crummey v. Commissioner, 397 F2d 82 (1968).

130 MCLA Section 449.1201.

131 MCLA Section 449.1303.

132 Subchapter K of the 1986 Code.

133 MCLA 450.4402.

134 MCLA Section 449.1303.

135 MCLA Section 450.4501(2).

136 MCLA Section 450.4101.

137 MCLA Section 449.1303.

138 Treasury Reg Section 25.2512.1.

139 Rev. Rul. 93-12, 1993-I-C.B. 202.

140 LeFrank v. Commissioner TC Memo 1993-526, 66 T.C.M. 1297 (1993); Private Letter Ruling 97-18-004 (5/2/97).

141 Estate of Andres v Commisioner, 79 T.C. 938 (1982).

142 IRC Section 2701 and 2702.

143 Mandelbaum v Commissioner, T.C. Memo 1995-225, 60 T.C.M. 2852 (1995).

144 /404(a)

145 Ten-year averaging (and capital gains on pre-1974 accumulations) are available on lump sum distributions if the participant was age 50 by January 1, 1986.

146 The term "participant" is used throughout this discussion to mean the owner of the account balance in the retirement plan.

147 Pre-age 59 1/2 distributions on account of the participant's death or total disability (along with a few other exceptions beyond the scope of this discussion) are exempt from the 10% tax.

148 Note that the Taxpayer Relief Act of 1997 eliminated the 15% excise tax that had applied to excess retirement plan accumulations.

149 /402(a)(7)

150 The Retirement Equity Act of 1984

151 IRC Section 170.

152 IRC Section 2055(a).

153 Qualifying charities are described in IRC Sections 2055(a) and 2522 (a).

154 IRC Section 664(c).

155 Treas. Reg. Section 1.664-1(a)(4).

156 IRC Section 664(b).

157 IRC Section 664(d)(1)(a).

158 Treas. Reg. 1.664-1(a)(a)(ii), Section Rev. Rul. 77-374, 1977-2 CB 329.

159 Treas. Reg. 1.664-2(b).

160 Treas. Reg. 1.664-2(a)(1)(iii).

161 IRC Section 664(d)(i)(D) and 664(d)(2)(D).

162 Gregory A. Schupra, "Assisting Clients in Charitable Giving: A Challenging Opportunity," Michigan Probate and Estate Planning Journal (Spring 1997).

163 Treas. Reg. Section 20.2055-2(e).

164 Private Letter Ruling 9431051.

165 IRC Section 664(d)(3)(A); Treas. Reg. Section 1.664-3-(a)(1)(b).

166 IRC Section 170(b)(1)(a).

167 IRC Section 170(b)(1)(D).

168 Id.

169 IRC Section 170(b)(1)(A).

170 IRC Section 170(b)(1)(C)(i).

171 IRC Section 170(d)(1) and Section 170(b)(1)(C)(iii).

172 IRC Section 170(e)(5).

173 The average U.S. life span is 77 years. U.S. Bureau of Census, Current Population Reports (1995).

174 USA Today, March 18, 1997.

175 42 CFR 409.30(a).

176 Id.

177 42 USC 1395(a)(2); 42 CFR 409.61 (b).

178 P.L. No. 104-191 (8/21/96), Sections 321-323, 325-26, amending Code Section 213 (d) and enacting Code Sections 4980C, 6050Q and 7702B.

179 IRC Section 213(d)(1)(D).
180 IRC Section 104(a).
181 P.L. No. 105-33, 111 State 251 at Section 4734.
182 PEM Item 400, Michigan Department of Social Services, Program Eligibility Manual ("PEM").
183 PEM Item 405, at 9.
184 Fractions of a month are not counted.
185 Advising the Older Client, (ICLE 1998). "Paying for Long-Term Care Costs," George A. Cooney, Jr., and David Shaltz.
186 PEM Item 401 at 8.
187 Omnibus Budget Reconciliation Act of 1993 (OBRA 1993), Section 1361 (a).
188 IRC Section 2613(a)(1).
189 IRC Section 2631(a).
190 IRC Section 2642(c)(2).
191 IRC Section 2612 (c).
192 IRC Section 2612(b).
193 IRC Section 2612(a)(1); Reg. 26.2612-1(b).
194 IRC Section 2631(a).
195 IRC Section 2652(a).
196 IRC Section 2652(a)(3).
197 IRC Section 2652(a)(2).
198 IRC Section 2642(a).
199 IRC Section 2642(a)(1).

Glossary

Adjusted gross estate	The value of all property owned by a decedent (valued on the date of death), less funeral expenses, the expenses of administering the estate, and debts owed by the decedent.
Alternate valuation date	A date, six months after the date of death, used to value property owned by the decedent. The alternate valuation date (sometimes known as the "AVD") may be used for estate tax purposes in cases where the value of the estate has declined in the six months following death.
Annual gift tax exclusion, or "annual exclusion"	The amount (currently $11,000 per donee) that can be excluded each year in computing the gift tax of the donor. Gifts in excess of the annual exclusion are taxable gifts that reduce the donors Unified Credit. Married couples may split gifts. See "Gift splitting" below.
Applicable Exclusion Amount	The total value of lifetime taxable gifts or transfers at death that can be transferred tax-free after application of the unified credit.
Basis	Term used in tax accounting to describe the cost of an asset for purpose of determining gain (or loss) on its sale or transfer. The starting point in calculating an owner's basis in an asset is to determine its original cost to the owner.

Beneficiary	A person who has any present or future interest, vested or contingent, under a Will, trust, retirement plan or life insurance policy.
By operation of law	The automatic change of title when one of multiple owners of property dies, such as joint tenants, P.O.D. or beneficiary designation. No court action is needed to transfer title.
Capital Gains Tax	A tax on the difference between the sales price and the adjusted basis of a capital asset. Long-term and short-term capital gains taxes are paid depending upon the length of time you have owned the asset.
Carry-over basis	The basis of the donor or decedent is transferred to and becomes the basis of the donee or beneficiary.
Closely Held Business	A privately held business in which stock is not publicly traded.
Conservator	A person appointed by the Court to exercise powers over the estate (financial matters) of a protected person.
Crummey notice	A notice sent to an irrevocable trust beneficiary to alert the beneficiary that a contribution has been made to a trust and the beneficiary has a right to obtain some or all of the contribution. Used to qualify the contribution as a "present interest" and qualify for the annual gift tax exclusion.
Disclaimer	A decision to not accept a gift or inheritance. Usually done for estate tax saving purposes.

Divestment	The process of transferring property to reduce your net worth in order to qualify for a means-eligible program like Medicaid.
Domicile	The permanent residence of a person or the place to which he or she intends to return even though he or she may actually reside elsewhere. A person may have more than one residence but only one domicile. The domicile of a person is important for state inheritance tax purposes and in determining the proper county to commence a probate estate.
Donee	The recipient of a gift.
Donor	One who makes a gift to another.
Dower	The life estate to which every married woman is entitled upon the death of her husband. In Michigan, surviving wives are entitled to a life estate in 1/3 of all the lands of her husband, at any time during the marriage. Men do not have Dower rights. See "Michigan Statutory Rights."
Durable powers of attorney	A written instrument whereby one person of attorney (the "principal"), appoints another person as his agent, with authority to perform certain acts on the principal's behalf. Powers of attorney are usually used to give an agent power to transact personal business if the principal is unable to do so directly. The term "durable" signifies that the power being granted continues to be effective despite the disability of the principal.
EPIC	Acronym for the "Estates and Protected Individuals Code," passed by the Michigan legislature which replaced the Revised Probate Code effective April 1, 2000.

Fiduciary	A person or institution who manages money or property for another and who is legally required to exercise a standard of care in such management activity. Trust fiduciaries are strictly bound to implement the terms of the trust instrument under which they are appointed.
General power of appointment	A power given the decedent by a third party to consume, invade or appropriate certain property in favor of the decedent, his estate or his creditors. Property over which the decedent possesses a general power of appointment at death is included in the decedent's gross estate for estate tax purposes.
Gift Splitting	A gift made by one spouse to any person other than his/her spouse where an election is made to consider the gift as having been made one-half by the donor and one-half by donor's spouse.
GRAT	Acronym for "Grantor Retained Annuity Trust." A GRAT is a trust to which the donor gifts property, but retains the right to receive equal (fixed) annual payments for a number of years specified by the donor.
Grantor	A person making a grant; the transferor of property. The creator of a trust is usually designated as the grantor of the trust. The term "settlor" is often used in the place of "grantor" since the terms are synonymous.
Gross estate	All property in which the decedent had a beneficial interest at the time of death. Examples include cash, stocks, bonds, real estate, business interests, and other tangible property.

GRUT	Acronym for "Grantor Retained Unitrust." A GRUT is a trust to which the donor gifts property, but retains the right to receive annual payments equal to a predetermined percentage of the trust property calculated annually based on the value of the trust's assets on the first day of the year.
Guardian	A person appointed by the court or designated as such in a Will to exercise powers over the person of a minor or legally incapacitated person.
Heir	Those persons, including the surviving spouse, who are entitled to the property of a decedent under the statutes of intestate succession.
ILIT	Acronym for "Irrevocable Life Insurance Trust." An ILIT is the owner and beneficiary of life insurance on the life of the grantor. Proceeds of the policy are not include ed in the estate of the grantor, and such trusts cannot be revoked or amended once created. See "Irrevocable Trust."
Incidents of ownership	Rights a person may have in a life insurance policy such as the right to name or change the beneficiary of the policy or the right to borrow from the policy.
Intestate	Term used to describe one who dies without leaving a valid Will.
IRD	Items of income earned by a decedent before death but paid to his or her estate after death. Such income is includible in the decedent's gross estate and is taxable income to the recipient. Examples of IRD include the decedent's last paycheck, interest on U.S. savings bonds, royalties, as well as IRA, 401(k) and other retirement income paid after death.

Irrevocable trust	A Trust (see "Trust" definition) created during the life of the grantor, under which the grantor gives up the right to amend or revoke the Trust, so that once created, the Trust cannot be altered. See "ILIT."
Joint tenants with rights of survivorship	A form of ownership that automatically vests ownership of a deceased joint owner's (tenant) share in the other joint tenants.
Joint Trust	A joint trust is a revocable grantor trust with two grantors-typically a husband and wife. Both spouses create the trust and transfer their assets to the trust. The trust normally provides that both spouses are the initial co-trustees and that the surviving spouse continues as the sole trustee, and retains the power to amend the trust after the first spouse's death.
Last Will and Testament	A legal declaration setting forth one's desires concerning the disposition of his or her property after death. Often simply referred to as a "Will."
Letters of authority	A document issued by the Probate Court giving the Personal Representative legal authority to transact the estate's business.
Limited Liability Company (LLC)	An entity created under state law, which (like a corporation) limits the potential legal liability of its owners to the amount they have invested in the LLC. Like a partnership LLCs pays no income tax, instead items of income and loss flow through to "members" who pay tax at their marginal income tax rate.
Limited Partnerships	A partnership consisting of at least one general partner who has unlimited liability and at least one limited partner who is liable for only the amount of his or her investment.

Marital trust	Trust into which trust assets in excess of the Applicable Exclusion Amount are allocated after the death of one spouse. All income and principal of the marital trust is available to the surviving spouse for her use. At death, of the surviving spouse may be permitted to designate the beneficiary of the balance of the Marital Trust (a "general power of appointment"), or may not ("QTIP" Trust).
Medicaid	A state-run health care program for individuals with low income and little or no resources. Eligibility is determined based on state guidelines. The state also determines which health care services are covered.
Medigap insurance	A private health insurance policy covering services not covered by Medicare.
Notice to creditors	The notice published in a legal newspaper notifying any and all potential creditors of the decedent's death and the time frame in which they must file their claims against the estate
Notice to known creditors	The notice sent directly to the decedent's known creditors to inform them of the death and the time frame for making claims against the estate
Pay-on-death	A type of beneficiary designation; pay-on-death (also, "P.O.D.") accounts are payable to the named beneficiary immediate on the account owner's death. Also known as "transfer-on-death," or "T.O.D." Typically used on brokerage accounts. Allows the account to pass by operation of law at the death of the primary owner to the beneficiaries named on the account. Only the owner can access the P.O.D or T.O.D. account while alive.

Personal property memorandum	A writing indicating the individuals who are to inherit particular items of the decedent's personal property, such as jewelry, collectibles and other family heirlooms.
Personal representative	A person, or committee of individuals, or a corporate fiduciary like a bank, appointed by the probate court, to administer the probate estate of a decedent. Sometimes also known as an "executor" or "executrix." The person named in the decedent's Will has first priority to be appointed as personal representative. If that individual is unable or unwilling to serve, or if the decedent died without a Will, the surviving spouse has first priority.
Pick-up tax	A type of state inheritance tax where the state receives a portion of the federal estate tax equal to the maximum state death tax credit available on the federal estate tax return.
Postnuptial agreement	An agreement entered into after marriage concerning the division of marital assets in the event of divorce or death; the agreement overrides state law with respect to such division.
Pour Over Will	A Will used in conjunction with a Revocable Living Trust, which serves as a safety net to transfer probatable assets into trust at death.
Prenuptial agreement	An agreement entered into before marriage concerning the division of marital assets in the event of divorce or death; the agreement overrides state law with respect to such division.

Present interest	The current right of a gift recipient (donee) to the unrestricted enjoyment of the gifted asset. To qualify for the annual gift tax exclusion, a gift must be of a present interest. A Crummey Notice is used to convert a future interest transfer to an irrevocable trust to a transfer of a present interest.
Probate	Generally, the process by which assets owned individually at death are transferred to the decedent's heirs; specifically, probate is court proceeding to authenticate the decedent's Will, appoint the personal representative, pay debts and taxes, identify heirs and distribute assets. A Will does not avoid probate; only a fully funded trust will obviate the necessity of probate.
Publication period	The period of time (usually four months) during which the decedent's creditors must file their claim against the estate, or else the claim is forever barred.
QTIP trust	Acronym for "Qualified Terminable Interest Property" Trust. A QTIP trust qualifies for the unlimited martial deduction if the surviving spouse has the exclusive right to income and principal from the trust during his/her lifetime. The surviving spouse cannot direct the disbursement of the balance of the QTIP Trust at his or her death.
Qualified pension and profit sharing plans	Retirement plans that comply with the federal Employee Retirement Income Security Act ("ERISA"); usually employer sponsored plans. Examples include company pension, profit sharing, and 401(k) plans.

Required minimum distribution	The minimum amount you must take annually from your retirement plan(s) beginning at age 70 1/2; the amount is calculated by dividing your retirement plan account balance (as of the previous December 31) by the Applicable Devisor from the IRS Uniform Table that corresponds to your age. If you have more than one IRA, 403(b), 401(k) or qualified plan, all like plans must be aggregated for purposes of meeting the RMD requirement.
Revocable Trust	A Trust (see "Trust") created during the Settlor/Grantor's life, under which the Settlor/Grantor retains the right to amend or revoke the Trust during his or her lifetime.
Rollover	A complete distribution taken from an IRA, 401(k) or other retirement plan which is then completely deposited into another IRA, 401(k), etc.
Special needs trust	A trust established for a beneficiary who is receiving means tested benefits like Medicaid or SSI, restricting transfers for the beneficiary's primary care so as to not disqualify the beneficiary from government benefits.
Specific bequest	A gift in a Will of particular items to a particular person. The gift must be of the item, not its value.
State death tax credit	A credit allowed by the Federal estate tax for estate or inheritance tax paid to a state.
Stepped up basis	An increase in the income tax basis of property held at death. Inherited property receives an income tax basis equal to its fair market value as of the date of the decedent's death. Items of IRD does not receive a stepped up basis.

Tangible Investment

Investments that have physical properties, such as gold and silver, stamps, coins and collectibles (e.g. artwork and sports memorabilia).

Tenancy by the entirety

A form of ownership of real property by a husband and wife, which is not recognized in all states. Unlike a joint tenant, one tenant's interest in a tenancy by the entireties cannot be separated from the interest of the other. If the parties divorce, they become tenants in common. Upon the death of the husband or wife, title goes to the survivor by operation of law.

Testate

Term used to describe one who dies leaving a valid Will.

Testator

One who makes a Will; one who dies leaving a Will.

Transfer-on-death

See "Pay-on-death."

Trust

A legal arrangement created under state law with three essential elements: 1) A Settlor/Grantor who establishes the Trust and who supplies the property for the Trust, 2) a Trustee who manages the property in the Trust, and 3) a Beneficiary, for whose benefit Trust property is held. A single person may occupy of these roles

Uniform Probate Code

A set of laws dealing with Wills, trusts, and probate, drafted by the National Conference of Commissioners on Uniform State Laws, to serve as a model for states that want to modernize their own laws on these subjects. In *Lost and Found*, we have used the Uniform Probate Code as the basis of our discussion. Unlimited marital deduction. This deduction allows spouses to make unlimited gifts or unlimited transfers to each other at death. Not available if the recipient spouse is not a U.S. citizen.

Warranty Deed

Deed in which grantor warrants or covenants good clear title. The usual covenants of title are warranties of seizen, quiet enjoyment, right to convey, freedom from encumbrances and defense of title as to all claims.

EXHIBIT A

DO-NOT-RESUSCITIATE ORDER

I have discussed my health status with my physician, _____. I request that in the event my heart and breathing should stop, no personal shall attempt to resuscitate me.

This order is effective until it is revoked by me.

Being of sound mind, I voluntarily execute this order, and I understand its full importance.

_____   _____

(Declarant's signature)   (Date)

_____

(Type or print declarant's full name)

_____   _____

(Signature of person who signed for   (Date)
declarant, if applicable

_____

(Type or print full name)

_____   _____

(Physician's signature)   (Date)

_____

(Type or print physician's full name)

ATTESTATION OF WITNESSES

The individual who has executed this Order appears to be of sound mind, an under no duress, fraud, or undue influence. Upon executing this Order, the individual has (has not) received an identification bracelet.

_____   _____

(Witness signature) (Date)   (Witness signature) (Date)

_____   _____

(Type or print witness name)   (Type or print witness name)

THIS FORM WAS PREPARED PURSUANT TO, AND IS IN COMPLIANCE WITH, THE MICHIGAN DO-NOT-RESUSCITATE PROCEDURE ACT

EXHIBIT B

ASSETS DECLARATION
PATIENT AND SPOUSE
Michigan Department of Social Services

FOR OFFICE USE ONLY			
Case Name			
Case Number			
County	District	Unit	Worker

PLEASE PRINT

Patient's Name (First, Middle, Last)		Phone No. of Nursing Home	Spouse's Name (First, Middle, Last)		Spouse's Phone Number
Address of Nursing Home (Number, Street, Rural Route)			Spouse's Address (Number, Street, Rural Route)		
City	State	Zip Code	City	State	Zip Code
Patient's Birthdate (Mo/Day/Yr)	Patient's Social Security Number		Spouse's Birthdate (Mo/Day/Yr)	Spouse's Social Security Number	

This form asks questions about the property or assets owned by you and/or your spouse. This information is needed to determine your eligibility for Medicaid and the amount of assets that can be protected for the benefit of your spouse.

Answer the following questions by providing information about all assets owned by you and/or your spouse as of _____ . Include assets you owned jointly with your spouse, family or other persons.

ASSETS

Do you and/or your spouse have any of the following? Each item must be answered YES or NO. Check yes even if the item is jointly owned. "Jointly owned" means your name and someone else's name is listed on the asset. For example, your name is not the only name listed on an account or on a registration or title to property.

	YES NO	Amount or Value		YES NO	Amount or Value
1. Cash on Hand or in a Safety Deposit Box	☐ ☐	$	11. Home	☐ ☐	$
2. Cash in a Patient Trust Fund	☐ ☐	$	12. Land or Buildings Other Than Your Home	☐ ☐	$
3. Savings Bonds	☐ ☐	$	13. Cars, Pick-Ups or Trucks	☐ ☐	$
4. Money Market Funds	☐ ☐	$	14. Other Vehicles such as Motor-homes, Campers, Boats, Trail-ers, Snowmobiles, Motorcycles	☐ ☐	$
5. IRA or KEOGH Accounts	☐ ☐	$	15. Mortgage or Land Contracts Payable to You	☐ ☐	$
6. Trust Funds	☐ ☐	$	16. Farm Equipment, Livestock, or Crops	☐ ☐	$
7. Stocks or Bonds or Any Account With a Stockbroker	☐ ☐	$	17. Tools and Equipment	☐ ☐	$
8. Notes or Contracts Payable to You	☐ ☐	$	18. Funeral Contract	☐ ☐	$
9. Life Insurance	☐ ☐	$	19. Burial Trust Funds	☐ ☐	$
10. Life Estate	☐ ☐	$	20. Burial Plots	☐ ☐	$

AUTHORITY: 42 CFR Part 435.
COMPLETION: Voluntary.
PENALTY: No Medicaid.

The Department of Social Services will not discriminate against any individual or group because of race, sex, religion, age, national origin, color, marital status, disability or political beliefs.

DSS-4574B (Rev. 3-94) Previous edition obsolete.

EXHIBIT B (continued)

ASSETS

COMPLETE THIS PAGE BY CHECKING YES OR NO OR WRITING IN THE ANSWER.

The Department of Social Services may check records with banks, credit unions, and savings and loans concerning any accounts that you may have. These accounts may be verified by computer cross-checking.

1. Is your name, or your spouse's name, on one or more checking accounts in any bank, credit union or savings and loan?
   ☐ YES   ☐ NO

2. Is your name, or your spouse's name, on one or more savings accounts or Certificates of Deposit in any bank, credit union or savings and loan?
   ☐ YES   ☐ NO

3. List each account, the name and address where the account is located, the account number and the balance in the account. Include all accounts, even those held jointly with other persons, those with small balances, Christmas clubs and accounts used for direct deposit. List the name of every person on the account.

CHECKING ACCOUNTS

Name(s) on the Account	Name and Address of Bank, Credit Union, or Savings and Loan	Account Number	Balance
A.			
B.			
C.			

SAVINGS ACCOUNTS OR CERTIFICATES OF DEPOSIT

Name(s) on the Account	Name and Address of Bank, Credit Union, or Savings and Loan	Account Number	Balance
A.			
B.			
C.			
D.			

4. Do you have an account that is not listed above?   ☐ YES   ☐ NO

5. Have you, your spouse or someone acting for either of you ever put any money, income, a lawsuit settlement or assets in a trust, annuity or similar device?   ☐ YES   ☐ NO

6. Do you have any other assets not already listed on this form?   ☐ YES   ☐ NO

If yes, explain: _____

AFFIDAVIT

I swear or affirm that all the information that I have written on this form or told to a caseworker is true. I understand that I can be prosecuted for perjury if I have intentionally given false information. I also know that I may be asked to show proof of any information I have given. I also know that if I have intentionally left out any information or if I have given false information, which causes me to receive assistance I am not entitled to or more assistance than I am entitled to, I can be prosecuted for fraud.

Signature (Patient or Authorized Representative)	Date (Month, Day, Year)

Two Witnesses Only If Signed by Mark **X**	Signature of First Witness	Signature of Second Witness

NOTE: If you are not an authorized representative but you helped complete this application, print your name and phone number where you may be reached.

Name (First, Middle, Last)	Phone Number

DSS-4574B (Rev. 3-94) (Back)

EXHIBIT C

ESTATE PLANNING QUESTIONNAIRE

GENERAL INFORMATION

Name _____

Other name known by (if any) _____

Address _____

Home Phone # _____

Work Phone # _____

SS# _____

Occupation _____

Date of Birth _____

Citizen of U.S.? _____

Other states or
Countries previously resided in _____

Have you entered into any
Pre-or Post-nuptial Agreements
(if so, attach copies) _____

Spouse's Name _____

Other name known by (if any) _____

Work Phone # _____

SS# _____

Occupation _____

Date of Birth _____

Citizen of U.S.? _____

Other states or
Countries previously resided in _____

Have you entered into any
Pre-or Post-nuptial Agreements
(if so, attach copies) _____

EXHIBIT C (continued)

Any prior marriages
(if divorced, year divorced;
if widowed, attach a copy of
Form 706 (tax return) for predeceased
Spouse's estate _____

Any prior marriages
(if divorced, year divorced;
if widowed, attach a copy of
Form 706 (tax return) for predeceased
Spouse's estate _____

CHILDREN
Rank the health, emotional and financial maturity of adult children (1 to 5, 1=greatest, 5=least)

Name	Age	Physical Health	Emotional Maturity	Financial Acumen	Married (M) Single (S) Divorced (D)	# of Children	City and State of residence

EXHIBIT C (continued)

WILLS & TRUSTS
Do you currently have a will? If so, when was it last updated? _____

A trust? If so, when was it created? _____

A Durable Power of Attorney? If so, when was it created? _____

An Irrevocable Trust (circle one)   Y   N;   A Family Limited Partnership or LLC?   Y   N;
A Charitable Remainder Trust?   Y   N

ASSETS AND LIABILITIES
Please list all of your assets and liabilities by category. Estimates are sufficient. Your figures need not be exact.

ASSETS	YOURS	SPOUSE'S	JOINT
Personal residence	$	$	$
Other Real Estate			
Life Insurance: (Total value of all policies)			
401(k)s, Pension, Profit Sharing			
IRAs			
Family Business (provide detail)			
Stocks/Stock Funds/Stock Options			
Other Marketable Securities			
Money Mark Funds			
Checking & Savings			
Annuities			
Collectible/Other Personal Assets			
TOTAL ASSETS	$	$	$

EXHIBIT C (continued)

FAMILY BUSINESS

Name of Business: _____   Nature of Business: _____

Address: _____

Indicated form of ownership (e.g., corporation, partnership, LLC, sole proprietorship): _____

Approximate value of business: _____

% of ownership: H: _____ W: _____ Children: _____
Original investment: H: _____ W: _____ Children: _____

Attach copies of buy-sell agreement relating to transfer of interests during lifetime or at death, employment agreements and financial statements.

LIABILITIES	YOURS	SPOUSE'S	JOINT
Personal debt (credit cards, lines of credit, etc.)	$	$	$
Home Mortgage			
Loans for Business and Partnership			
Auto Loans			
Other Short-Term Debt			
Real Estate Mortgage			
Other Long-Term Debt			
TOTAL LIABILITIES	$	$	$
NET ESTATE	$	$	$

EXHIBIT C (continued)

SURVIVING PARENT INFORMATION

YOUSELF

Parents Ages: Father: _____

Mother: _____

Estimated size of Estate: _____

Number of siblings: _____

Any special circumstances or family relationships
that may affect plan of disposition of assets at death?

_____

_____

SPOUSE

Parents Ages: Father: _____

Mother: _____

Estimated size of Estate: _____

Number of siblings: _____

Any special circumstances or family relationships
that may affect plan of disposition of assets at death?

_____

_____

CHARITABLE BEQUESTS

Are there any Charitable entities you wish to remember upon your death? (circle one)   Y   N

If so, please list:

_____

_____

COMMENTS: _____

Index

grantor retained annuity trust 58
grantor retained unitrust 58
gross estate 15
Guardian 9

- H -
Health Insurance Portability and Accountability Act of 1996 119
homestead allowance 79

- I -
Incidents of ownership 16, 86
Inclusion Ratio 129
income in respect of a decedent 68
independent appraiser 18
informal probate 40
intestate 30
inventory fee 42
inventory 42
IRA 51
irrevocable trusts 11

- J -
joint tenancy 35
joint tenants with rights of survivorship 35
joint trusts 72
jointly held assets 17

- L -
letters of authority 40
life estate 57
life insurance 51
life support 21
Limited Liability Company 60, 92
long term care 117
LTC 117
lump sum distribution 98

- M -
marginal tax rate 58
marital trust 18
marketability discount 94